WITHDRAWN

P9-ARB-577

DATE DUE

JUN 19 1986

AUG 28 1986

AUG 30 1986

OCT 18 1986

Art for Teachers of Children

MERRILL'S INTERNATIONAL SERIES IN EDUCATION

Kimball Wiles, *Editor*
University of Florida

Chandler Montgomery

New York University

Art for Teachers of Children

Foundations of aesthetic experience

CHARLES E. MERRILL PUBLISHING COMPANY

Columbus, Ohio   *A Bell and Howell Company*

Copyright © 1968 by Charles E. Merrill Publishing Company, Columbus, Ohio. All rights reserved. No part of this book may be reproduced, by mimeograph or any other means, without the written permission of the publisher.

Library of Congress Catalog Card Number: 68-10088

68 69 70 71 72 73 74 / 10 9 8 7 6 5 4 3 2 1

Printed in the United States of America

Copy 2

NX
282
.M66
Copy 2

Illustration Acknowledgments

The author and the publisher would like to acknowledge and thank the following individuals and companies for their efforts and cooperation in supplying us with, what we feel, are illustrations of superior quality and interest.

From Richard Bluestein, the Frontispiece and Figures 44, 50, 67, 68, 70, 75, 80, 82, 98, 103, 104, 105, and 106.

From the Green Shoe Manufacturing Company, Figure 52, "A Child's Path from Home to School."

From Burt Chernow, Figure 62 which represented the United States in a UNESCO exhibit at the United Nations pavilion at the New York World's Fair, 1964-65, and appeared in a United States Information Agency world traveling exhibit.

The remainder of the photography was done by Christopher Montgomery, son of the author.

We would also like to thank the young women who served as models for those photos illustrating sculptural form and the potentials of working with clay.

Author's Acknowledgments

The emphasis of this book on "what goes on" in the thinking-feeling processes of art work has grown out of teaching experiences in outstanding schools, especially the public schools of Winnetka, Illinois. Here it was assumed that the interests and concerns of children, wherever they occurred, might be sources of creative expression. Similar convictions enlivened a series of workshops for teachers, beginning at Northwestern University and later continued at New York University, including summers in Springfield, Missouri, in Athens, Georgia, and in Puerto Rico.

Naming the individuals who have enriched these teaching-learning years is impossible, but there are some who have contributed directly to this writing venture. Among these are Lillian Kiesler, Ivan Johnson, Mary Giles and other colleagues in the art program of the Division of Early Childhood and Elementary Education, at New York University. Many of the experiments grew out of an interdepartmental teaching venture in Related Arts. This course began with Gladys Andrews and Hale Woodruff as fellow explorers, and it has continued to develop with a growing list of artist-teachers and consultants whose ideas have influenced this book.

The writing itself depended throughout on the counsel and encouragement of Elizabeth, my wife. Another critical reader was Christopher, my son who made almost all of the photographs. Richard Bluestein's skill in capturing the quality of children's actions is shown in fourteen photographs, and another was contributed by art teacher Bert Chernow. Finally, special thanks are due to Julia Estadt of Charles E. Merrill Publishing Company for her skill and understanding as production editor.

Chandler Montgomery

Contents

Observing and recording the shape of living: movement in floor space, levels. Experiments in space modification: use of flat, curved, or irregular planes in space structures; clay slab shells. Experiment within a given volume: the space box. Building space awareness with blocks.

Providing conditions favorable to aesthetic-creative experience: 1) *permitting,* through time, choice; 2) *inviting,* through planning, direct sensing; 3) *focusing,* through finding, selecting, continuing; 4) *supporting,* through self-help, self-evaluation.

1

Introduction

A teacher friend, hearing plans for this book, said it sounded "like a combination cookbook and prayer book." The cooks, bless them, would probably disagree. To them "art for teachers of children" would mean things which teachers could show children how to make or do. It might also include instructions on ways to work, although that would be getting over into the "prayer" department. To the extent that we adults may see teaching children as a limited job, overlaying but not deeply involving *ourselves,* the challenge to refresh our own seeing so that we can help children may seem indirect and less desirable than a series of activities planned and ready to serve to children.

Art experience as an element of children's education has been undergoing attacks from outside and reductions from inside the teaching profession. In schools where art is now listed as a regular part of curriculum there is often a great gap between theoretical pronouncements and actual classroom practices. Instead of an exciting and demanding experience with fundamental processes, a stultifying reduction-for-children of bodies of knowledge seems to occur in many areas of curriculum, not only in art; such reduction seems to accompany teaching done by both classroom teachers and subject specialists.

Being aware of the vacuum left by the extension of objectively impersonal, technologically-oriented curricula, a sensitive teacher will covet for children the more basic discipline of honest, purposeful play with materials—physical, psychological, and social materials—and the individual, moral responsibility of stating "how I see it."

This book proposes that focusing on aesthetic experience will help to counteract reducing tendencies in education and will open up new learning possibilities, both for the teacher and for the children he teaches. The difference such experience brings to any learning (again, not only art) is qualitative and must be achieved through personal sensing and constructive involvement. The result can be a kind of insight and conviction capable of changing behavior, including the teacher's.

Recipes, lists, and instructions can be helpful aids to teachers and children. They can also lead to a kind of isolated production experience, to be recalled later as, "We had that last year with Miss Jones." When such instructions really help, it is because the teacher is able to read between the how-to lines to see Johnny's grin and Maria's consternation. This ability to read children's thinking/feeling process between the lines of art work comes from experience more personal than lesson planning.

Most of us have had the special experience of learning in the companionship of a teacher who, along with his knowing and loving a certain field, wanted to find and was able to find ways by which *we* could be inducted into it. To what extent it was his knowing the field or his knowing us that made his teaching memorable is a much discussed professional question, but it is less critical than the fact that he brought to his teaching, and to us, a high quality of knowing. The great teacher of children needs deep roots in experience if he is to bring the distilled quality of his living into that productive relationship with children's living which is the essence of teaching.

In addressing teachers of children we are thinking primarily of those who are specialists, or are interested in becoming specialists, in pre-school and elementary classroom teaching; but we also have in mind those other workers-with-children who bring to teaching a rich experience in the arts or other specialized fields.

Unlike most adults, teachers of children frequently observe clear differences in expressive behavior, from deeply felt wonder to evasiveness or withdrawal; they may sense when a child is personally involved in his work and when he is only busy. If, in spite of this, their teaching of art, for example, remains a combination of step-by-step directions and puzzled permissiveness, the reasons may be found less in their educational intentions than in their trained disconnection of directly sensed, personally felt experience from any kind of learning, including art learning. The prayerbook purpose of this book, then, is to re-establish this basic connection where it has been broken by self-doubt, and to renew and enrich it where the flow has dwindled from disuse. Teachers, after all, must be personally involved in creative experience before they can effectively guide others to it.

In purported defense of academic standards in liberal/cultural studies, institutions of higher learning have been moving away from studio work with art materials, at least for non-specialists in art, sometimes substituting lectures on art history or art appreciation. Professional courses on teaching methods are also being cut down to allow for specialization in an academic field within the elementary program, leaving more direct art experiences to art specialists. This book attempts to present a broadening alternative to this narrowing trend. It undertakes to use the reader's "studio time" well, provoking many questions in limited hours of work with materials, and realizing that the importance of the questions depends on the depth of personal venture which they represent.

It would be unrealistic to hope that reading this book would affect patterns of experiencing if this reading led only to a muttering of sideline cheers and protests about art. Our analysis and argument, therefore, do not seek the reader's full agreement so much as they try to enlist his active, independent participation in many kinds of first-hand experiments in sensing, responding, and inventing.

The plan of the book is to present a series of working situations, each selected to clarify or highlight a certain type of *aesthetic experience* (as with texture, color, or sound), inviting four kinds of response in the reader:

1. Individual ventures with suitable materials to externalize one's own aesthetic experience.
2. Searching out and observing this type of aesthetic experience as it occurs in the unorganized environment.
3. Study of its purposeful transformation in masterworks, works of art.
4. Reading, discussion, thinking about, and projecting extensions and applications of this kind of experience to other situations, such as the variations of children's needs and interests.

Producing art (or artists) is not the aim of this approach. It is rather to develop an appetite or preference for what is lively, vivid, and personally felt.

Most of the experiments suggested are fairly simple to set up and to carry through. The companionship of fellow students and the skilled guidance of teachers will help to multiply ideas and responses and to enlarge insights into the meanings of working process. However, most of the experiments could be done alone or with those who might frequent the home workroom or kitchen. Much of the work should take place not inside any studio but "out and around" in the environment and also, with luck and some effort, in the presence of works of art.

The fact that most of the supplies and equipment called for are the ones children use in school should not be misconstrued. In planning certain kinds of direct sensing, selecting, and organizing, there is of course no assumption that the adult will respond as children respond. On the other hand the insights which he may gain into the *kinds* of conditions which help or hinder him can be translated into a more sensitive understanding of children's learning processes. In some cases suggestions for adaptations to children's use in the classroom are included in the Appendix. Actually, the reader likely will be able to translate "things for children to do" out of his own working experience, combined with his knowledge of children. But sharing the pleasure of one's own doing is quite different from administering the prescription of a lesson plan.

Work which requires previous technical mastery of media has been avoided, while allowing for possible achievement and the development of even virtuoso skills. It is hoped that working with the questions introduced here will whet the appetite for more extensive and intensive study. Resources suitable for this purpose are suggested.

How far the reader is to carry the experiments, argue the theoretical questions, or follow through to study the environment and works of art will depend, of course, on his interest; it will also measure insights to be gained. Both aesthetic experience and creative work, which form the content of this book, must be sought and grasped by the individual. Our aim then is to provide conditions which will help the reader to have his own creative/aesthetic experience and, in turn, to provide conditions favorable for children's learning.

SECTION I

The Lively Difference

The work of the teacher of children has always proven more interesting than the assignment spelled out in contracts or the expectations of many teachers themselves. The main directives of that assignment are clear enough: to train children in skills of communication, logical thinking, conceptualizing, generalizing, measuring, predicting, and so on, and to lead them in more or less detail through various exhibits of the heritage they are to carry on.

Beyond the Assignment

The part of the teacher's work which is harder to "program" and to test is suggested by the child's tone of voice and facial expression as he tells what he does in school. Here may be signs of individual involvement, curiosity, liking, and independent inquiry, expressed in fumbling impatience, laughter, eagerness, open-eyed surprise, or quiet preoccupation. Or the signs may suggest beginnings of a kind of utilitarian know-how, such as, "Is this the kind of answer you want?"

Every teacher is necessarily subject to two different kinds of pressures. One is to get things done, that is, to get enough tasks performed well enough in a system of measurable educational production. The other is to develop the talents of children, helping them to realize their individual potential for growth and learning. We know that educational management requires simplification or reduction of many kinds of differences. The question is whether this reduction is looked upon as the desired goal or as an arrangement of the setting to enable development of unforeseen but prized differences. For many reasons we come to have an emotional stake either in tying things up in summarized packages or in opening things up as new possibilities—not only for children but for ourselves.

What happens in a classroom can range all the way from the doped dullness of rote learning to the sudden ecstasy of revelation—again, not only for the children, but for the teacher as well. Neither end of that range is the exclusive domain of any group of children or adults, of any one subject area in the curriculum, or of any one way of working or teaching. Indeed, most of us can remember a kind of electrical excitement accompanying the artificial, single-focused competition of classroom drill under the direction of an impersonal drill master. There one experiences the suppression of individual differences to conform to an outside model. But more than that, the experience is directed toward the joy of getting rather than the joy of knowing. Taken regularly it can become the kind of drug which, for all its excitement, leads to dullness.

How much the striving for correct answers affects a child depends on the sturdiness he has achieved as an experiencing individual. If certain achievements make him feel that he is "somebody," he could also become "nobody" by the same standards. On the other hand, he may have a background of trying many things on his own. These ventures may have led to all kinds of interesting developments, including "correct" answers but also adding to the inner and outer resourcefulness of himself as a tested, experienced individual—a person.

Degrees and Kinds of Involvement

Whoever has observed children, or indeed himself, knows the lively difference between resigned obedience and the assertive, infinitely variable processes of sensing, reaching out for, and taking all kinds of things, including the most abstract generalizations, and making them one's own. These are the processes of aesthetic experience and creative work. In simple forms these processes are a natural part of childhood, but the eroding demands of growing up reduce their effect on most adults, including teachers.

Most of us have had an opportunity to observe an infant playing. Lying in his crib, he smiles back at us, squeezing out a wet bubble from between his lips. His

1   *Involvement.*

legs curl upward, then thrash vigorously up and down with arms echoing their movement. His head turns to one side, his mouth finds a thumb, and his other hand gently kneads a fold in the blanket.

What goes on here? No doubt there would be ways to test whether the baby was more interested in the bubble than in us; whether the kicking was further celebration of his birth or reaction to the moist warmth of diapers; whether the concentration on the thumb included the kneading with the other hand but excluded us, and so on. We could break down the baby's behavior into smaller propositions to help us know more about it. On the other hand, we might also share the mother's kind of knowing of the baby as a radiating center of wholeness within living time and space.

Here our attention could be sidetracked from the baby to consider different kinds of observing, and we could argue about scientific method versus poetic imagination. Certainly there might be a kind of solid reassurance in counting the baby's right-left thumb preference or in reading electrical instruments taped on the mother; and the clearly communicable results of such study might support pride in the claim, "We now know that. . . ." On the other hand, the mother's kind of knowing includes and gives meaning to the gains of technology. However, if others are to share the mother's insights they must take a less factual, more subjective viewpoint.

To observe a baby is to observe ourselves without the conflicting overlay of experience. And questions follow, such as how one's action combines the "inside" and the "outside," and how it reverberates across the elusive boundary between "me" and "not me."

The baby also reminds us how more or less of one's total being may be invested in an action. At one point his kicking tenses even the muscles around his eyes, so that all of him is kicking; but the rhythm of his fingers curling is tied only loosely to the rhythm of sucking. Years later in reading a book his hand will turn a page. This action, beautiful in its economy, will call on fingers, wrist, and even arm and shoulder. His head will turn slightly, and the purposeful line of his reading will speed on past the scenery of its rich support.

What is Aesthetic Experience?*

The dictionary tells us that the aesthetic "pertains to the beautiful, as distinguished from the moral and, especially, the useful." By focusing our attention on aesthetic *experience* we can see beauty not as some kind of internal or external state, but as a dynamic quality in our changing, developing responses and responsiveness.

Aesthetic experience begins with and depends on the senses; as it continues it results in more acute sensory perception. However, our primary purpose in encouraging response to finer differences is not to produce such specialists as the tea taster or the color matcher, valuable though they are, but to increase the individual's contact with the possibilities of what lies before him—possibilities for his own enjoyment to use and share through creative construction. Thus aesthetic experience is not confined to the discriminatory functioning of the individual's sensory-nervous system; it includes such emotional responses as enjoyment, wonder, and the dedication of all levels of one's consciousness to an action.

The goal of aesthetic experience is a full, rich life for the individual. This purpose goes beyond the utilitarian, "Can you eat it, can you sell it?" Indeed, aesthetic experience is specifically "useless"; but in terms of larger human values it is criti-

---

*This section is adapted from the author's chapter, "Sensing and Responding to the World: Aesthetic Development" in *Curriculum for Today's Boys and Girls,* Robert S. Fleming, ed. (Columbus, Ohio: Charles E. Merrill Books, Inc., 1963).

cally useful. It is weakened or subverted by such ulterior motives as desire for applause, social approval, prizes, grades or pay. In this it is like love, which must be given freely rather than be bargained for. In practice our motives are often less pure than this ideal; hence, our aesthetic experience is often only an aspect of complex behavior, just as love is often only an aspect of complex human relationships.

It is important to distinguish between aesthetic experience and experience aimed at what is commonly called good taste. One could exhibit such approved taste without having any aesthetic experience simply by conforming to dicta of various authorities in order to be in fashion, compete with others, or be inconspicuous. By contrast, aesthetic experience *demands* taste: tasting, savoring, enjoying out of interest and good appetite. It means working with one's own perceptions of qualitative, sensed differences. From this working comes the aesthetic quality of one's planning, changing, choosing, and evaluating.

Our concern is with the individual's aesthetic experiencing—his own active, doing process—rather than with comparison of his products with standards of good taste. Without this emphasis on process, we may make quite false assumptions concerning the aesthetic development of others with backgrounds different from our own. Today we are involved in many kinds and degrees of integration. If "good taste" becomes more important to us than "more life," this integration process can lead to dull conformity and a dangerous waste of human resources.

The infant's aesthetic development is helped by settings of comparative quiet and security, free from attack and distraction by self-appointed, well-intentioned stimulators, on the one hand, and from brutalized competitors for survival, on the other. Later, as he develops, this security can include a remarkable range of apparent confusion and noise, leading to important aesthetic experience within situations of conflict and even violence.

More than retention of innocence has taken place between the young child's enjoyment of a music box and the adult's response to structural interplay in a string quartet. Child and adult share one essential: they both like music. Each feels he has a right to hear it as himself, with his own individual experience. The adult has not decided that this is for experts only and not for him.

Any aesthetic sensing is a form of action, but it can vary from vague awareness, almost passive in exposure, to active choice and statement of preferences in some form of personal construction. This full range of responding is open to and is used by most of us. Where individuals are limited, by emotional disturbance, to hazy distortions of environmental reality, careful study is being given to methods of increasing their contact with and pleasure in the world around them.

Others limit their responses by various kinds of selective preoccupation, like the ten-year old boy who entered a crowded room looking for one of his friends and left to report, "There's no one there." However, when response, going beyond simple recognition, includes reaching out, taking, and working with aesthetic qualities and then incorporating personal experience in the invention of new form, aesthetic experience approaches the more complete action of creative process.

The word creative has suffered from promiscuous use. Since we are seeking insights into processes of aesthetic experience and creative work, we shall need to outline what we mean by creative work.

What is Creative Work?

Creative work is a statement of preferences or considered choices based on both intuitive and rational experience with materials, and bringing into existence an organization of these materials in a form which is therefore unique, new, or original.

Such a ponderous definition needs explanation. It describes work which goes beyond problem solving of the deliberate, logical, step-by-step kind and is also different from whimsical carelessness. Its uniqueness is based on its inclusion of "preconscious," intuitive, individual experience with materials. The *materials* thus included are not only the things, but also the many kinds of relationships one may find to work with. We shall investigate "materials" and "experience with materials" in the next chapter.

The requirement that creative work bring into existence a form, organization, or statement means that it goes beyond inconclusive wishing and daydreaming, although these may play an important part in its preparatory phases. It should also be able to evoke a response or to say something to others. Historically, many products of creative work, later judged great, at first found no audience prepared to understand them; so they were then only potentially communicative. It should be noted that many other "creative" products proved to communicate little or nothing, then or now.

Such a description of creative work begins to differentiate it from other, less personal kinds of work. It is general enough to apply to both artistic (expressional) and to scientific or technological (problem solving) kinds of creative work.

What is Creative Process?

Descriptions of creative process, constructed from much testimony by and observation of creative people in many fields, include two predominant parts: (1) all that goes into the *discovery* of the idea, plan, or solution; and (2) all that goes into the *working out,* elaboration, or verification of that plan or idea. It will be seen that these two phases differ in character: the first requiring much imaginative, speculative play; the second, more skills, logical analysis, and evaluation.

The discovery phase of creative process is generally reported to consist of several parts or aspects. First, there is a more or less prolonged period of preparatory play. This may have begun unnoticed in idle speculation, moving on to some kind of direct questioning, not necessarily verbalized. If the questions raised are easily answered or "figured out" by methods of logical problem solving, there is no need to call on the more demanding processes of creative work. If, however, the preparatory play devel-

2   *Beginnings of aesthetic experience.*

ops into persistent, concentrated searching for an elusive plan, idea, or solution that "feels right," the questioning may lead to baffled puzzlement. Artists and scientists report that they have often had to put such questions aside in frustration or defeat. If the search had been seriously begun, it continues "on the back burner" of the subconscious and may produce, by an intuitive leap, the "flash of insight" which is the new, original, creative idea. Its newness or originality results from the unique individual life experience tapped in the searching process, as we noted in our definition of creative work.

It is our purpose in succeeding chapters to look into the nature of this process of creative play and to suggest ways of trying it out in a series of experiments. We recognize the difference in scale and quality between our part-time efforts and the life-time dedication which can lead artists and scientists to great discovery and invention. But we can retain the main requirement, namely, to give ourselves generously to playing with possibilities so that we may discover our own plans or ideas.

Especially in art expression, this play aspect of creative work must draw on as much of our thinking/feeling experience as we can open up to it. The idea of play is often associated commercially with "new," "easy," and "fun," thus promising novelties, quick results, and "a laugh a minute." Nevertheless, most children and their teachers sense that creative play is not to be confused with the titillation of being entertained. In the search for one's own ideas, setting out to be clever or different is no substitute for straightforward, individual integrity.

The other large part of the creative process—working out a discovered, personal idea or hunch—tends to allow more direct, controlled action. One must realize his envisioned goal. This usually calls for applying skills, carrying out constructive processes, and making necessary modifications, revisions, or completely fresh starts until the plan is realized. In practice, of course, the creative process may differ tremendously from any theoretical formulations. Autobiographies of creative individuals testify to this.

Even this brief review of the creative process will suggest to teachers where much so-called creative work with children falls short* and where much adult work, in arts and crafts, for example, is not really creative. The search for one's own plan or organization, based on one's own thinking and feeling experience, is often by-passed in favor of a ready-made plan, imposed in the form of demonstrations, standards, or models of end products. What remains is only to carry out the steps of producing or "creating" this predetermined product. It is sometimes noted that such producing is "new" if one has not done it before, but novelty of experience should not be confused with the depth of experience brought to the search for form in creative work.

Creative work does result in organized statements. These statements, especially in the visual arts, provide us with manageable objectifications of our choices, and for this reason they play an essential role in our self-education in creative process. They are also potentially communicative, as we have noted; and in a world of practical adjusting where the slogan "It's the results that count" is commonly accepted, the individual responsibilities of creating tend to be forgotten in the business of grinding out acceptable products.

A different hazard for most adults is that they suffer from years of trained spectatorship on the aesthetic sidelines. From a safe distance they can "know about" everything; but their responding rarely demands that they commit themselves in organized statements of individually held choices: "I see, I like, I say." Such commitment is very different from opinionated passing of judgments. In fact, creativity may be described as preferring to work with possibilities rather than passing judgments—for example, bringing out children's talents rather than measuring and grouping them.

The "considered preferences and individually held choices" of creative work are very different from the decisions reached by the objective analysis of most problem

---

*See Appendix, p. 175.

solving because in creative work they draw upon much more than the top layers of consciousness. The degree of commitment in "I like" can be much more than that in "I vote yes."

The ability to participate generously, without self-consciousness, is part of great teaching. As teachers we have sensed this difference occasionally in our own experience. Participation in art has a special power to call forth this quality of individual response and identification. While finding new aesthetic possibilities in the world around us, we also discover new capacities within ourselves for enjoyment and spontaneous behavior. And these capacities improve our companionship with children in their discovery of themselves.

Earlier we explained the double nature of this book's plan. In succeeding chapters the "prayer book" aspect, set in standard, full measure type, re-examines some of the simpler but often overlooked processes of aesthetic seeing and saying. But along with these inquiries, its "cook book" aspect, set in boldface, narrow measure type, invites the reader to take part in a series of working experiments, open-ended but focused on different processes of aesthetic experience and creative work. They ask him to engage in certain kinds of adult play without benefit of admirable end products or of art activities to be taught "as is" to children. The goal is more basic: increased teacher participation in individual aesthetic/creative experience.

Questions

1. How can a teacher become more sensitive to children's creative process?
2. What phases of creative process do teachers often omit, cut short, or overemphasize? Why? What is the effect on the continuing work of the child? How can this be changed?
3. How may teaching itself be creative work?

3

The Process of Finding Materials

It is interesting to watch people moving along a street and to observe what they are noticing especially or stopping to examine. We know that these visible signs of interest may be poor indicators of what is really taking place, and if pushed to explain the working process we would probably hedge our guesses with "It all depends." Professional observers would make similar reference to situational factors which affect looking and seeing, and they might go on to study the individual's external and internal situations. Others, accustomed to commercial "communicating," might see traps set to snare the attention of passersby; their electric signs and loudspeakers becoming city versions, or perversions, of nature's bright petals and plumage.

What Part of Looking and Seeing is Taken and What Part of It Is Given?

How do one's external and internal situations match up? We have noted the young child's special ability to respond openly to the world around him. Something catches his eye and he stops to look, to touch, to pat, poke, pick up, taste, and so on.

Elaborate physical processes, such as eye focus and convergence, are brought into play in complex operations analyzed by neurologists, biologists, psychologists, and other students of human functioning and development. While our concern with aesthetic experience and creativity may draw us into these fields in many instances, we are looking at different questions. For example, do we believe we are passive victims of our environment or effective participants in it?

How Can You Change a Thing or a Stuff into Usable Material?

The child's looking, selecting, trying out, and enjoying are part of discovery and play. He is busy combining his own experience with perceived qualities of the environmental thing, to "make it his own." If one thinks of any material as something to work with, a material for aesthetic experience would need to offer some special sensory qualities which would attract the individual and evoke in him an active, personal response. While we ordinarily think of such materials as visible, physical things, we know they may also be other kinds of phenomena, such as sounds, spaces, or kinds of relationships.

What Are "Found Materials"?

The term "found material" is commonly applied to a thing or a stuff for which some new, unexpected use has been discovered, especially in the arts. Often there is an added implication of salvaging what has been rejected, as in "waste materials," and perhaps of saving money by substituting the found for the bought. In this book our focus on aesthetic and creative *experience* results in a special emphasis on the process of finding; and the material is "found" in terms of individual sensory response to its aesthetic qualities and creative possibilities.

What Kinds of Things Are Most Likely to Become Materials for Aesthetic/Creative Work?

Remembering that materials are made useful by responses of individuals, we may note some characteristics of stuffs which tend to affect their potential as materials:

1. *Accessibility to Sensory Exploration:* for example, can you see it, hear it, pick it up, touch it, handle it, smell it, move it, or move yourself in relation to it?

2. *Workability:* for example, can you turn, twist, bend, cut, color, mark, tear, or fasten it? In other words, can you change and control it without elaborate, indirect, manipulative maneuvers?

3. *Variability in Relationship:* for example, does it bring some clarity of character to interplay with setting or with associated materials? Can it be adapted or modified to behave differently in such interplay or does it always sing the same solo? Can it perform effectively in repetition, recurrence, varied concentration, subordination, or featuring?

Beyond these general kinds of differences, stuffs appeal differently to the tastes of individuals and of groups. Since these tastes reflect experience, they can be modified. The difference between taste which is rooted in individual aesthetic experience and "good" taste, with is applicability for ulterior motives, was discussed in Chapter 2. If teachers are conscious of the sources and development of their own tastes, they will understand the importance of including the kinds of things to work with which will be most helpful in the aesthetic development of children. The children themselves are, of course, the best source of this information. While working with found materials in the classroom they will offer to an attentive teacher not only a list of things they like but, more importantly, insight into the thinking and feeling processes which underlie the selection and which may point the way to a different, but "right," list of things for them to move on to.*

The teacher who spends an exchange year working with children in another part of the world may find himself asking, "Why do they want to work with our ugly, machine-made stuff instead of those lovely things growing just outside the door?" Being a teacher, rather than a dealer in things, his concern and his satisfaction will center in the complex processes by which people "find" things and convert them into life-giving materials.

What Are Different Ways of Responding to Things?

Unlike young children, adults bring a great range of experience to the act of perceiving things and trying out their possibilities as materials. This experience may be expressed in:

1. *Quick dismissal* of things as failing to meet one's needs and interests, either because they are obviously inappropriate or because they are too familiar— "nothing new here, old stuff, boring, earlier experience has exhausted it"; or because they are too unfamiliar—"things look too complicated, obscure, inaccessible, requiring special background to understand." In either case experience leads to passing by—"name, file, and forget."

---

*Methods of organizing found materials for children's art activities are discussed in the Appendix, p. 177.

2. *Attentive, analytical questioning,* based on experience in systematic classification and sustained, logical examination of objectively verifiable relationships, such as cause and effect. Others equally well trained would respond in much the same way.

3. *Open, confident curiosity,* or generally good appetite, based on past experiences which were personally satisfying enough to promise a good chance of success in new finding. "What's this? I'll give it a try."

4. *Sensuous fascination or enjoyment,* or a feeling of identification with certain stuffs or objects. This is the experience of hitting upon possible constructions out of playful liking rather than logical analysis. Others would respond similarly to the extent that their thinking/feeling experience overlapped.

As experienced finders none of us approaches his environment in only one of these ways. Both the second and the fourth of these approaches probably depend on and grow out of the third's "confident curiosity" or an expectation that interesting possibilities, of one kind or another, may be found. It should be noted that something like the first-named "quick dismissal" could play an essential part in the selective focusing of attention required for the other kinds of response. But one crucial difference would be present: the exclusion would be a *tentative* dismissal. On the basis of "confident curiosity," one would say, or more accurately, feel, "While I choose to work with only this material now, I am sure that in different situations I would find these other things could also become materials." The right to such assurance is earned —or not earned, or denied—in many testing, looking ventures, small and large. Especially within a classroom group, with all its exciting variations, a child may need help to select and to focus on those materials which will offer him the best working experience at that time.

Where Are Materials Found?

Materials may be found among the random possibilities in a comparatively unknown, unplanned setting. "I was just looking around and I happened to come across . . ." Such a setting may *extend* the finding by introducing unexpected materials, especially if members of a group join in the hunt. (As we shall note, close observation of such an open environment—a stretch of sandy beach, for example— often shows a kind of order or consistency within the apparently random occurrence of its elements.)

On the other hand, one may find materials among possibilities which have been previously selected by oneself or others to focus on, emphasize, or clarify a certain kind of experience: "Here, for example, are some things like what I'm looking for." Such a narrowed setting may help to *intensify* the finding experience, increasing the finder's response to the way the material behaves so that within the interactions the

"I" of the finder plays a more decisive part than the "it" of the material. Such pre-selection will probably show that related materials help extend working possibilities better than do large quantities of materials. Thus it is usually easier to choose a surface with the right texture from a collection of textured surfaces rather than from a box of "everything." But more importantly, the choice will probably be much more discriminating, especially if one has helped with the collecting and sorting.

Who Finds Materials?

The special pleasure in running across something unexpected in an unlikely setting can favor later work with it. "It was just lying there until I came along," is a different beginning from, "What does she see in this stuff?" But neither approach would necessarily limit the extent to which one might eventually make it one's own found material.

Even if "she" represents the kind of authority which makes the plans, prescribes the ingredients and predetermines the outcomes of obedient work, one may still snatch moments of personal finding. But the officially approved possibilities of materials will tend also to predict the possibilities of the working experience.

Of course, no healthy individual surrenders all of his independence and responsibility when he hears, "Do as I say!"—at least not until the rewards, punishments, and other accompaniments have come to temper the command. Nor can faith in oneself be expected to develop automatically. It grows out of successes in meeting challenging personal ventures which are, or come to be, self-assigned. In this sense each individual must learn to find his own materials.

Does this mean that other, experienced people cannot help the finder narrow down his choice of working materials? Should a teacher, as an experienced "other" person, choose materials for the student, who is the individual "experiencer"? Should the teacher work with the student at first, and then leave him to proceed with his own choosing? The latter kind of intervention and help is probably most needed by habitual "dismissers." Such people, including most adults, need to rediscover possibilities for aesthetic satisfaction in materials and, even more, in themselves.

Developing Purposeful Direction

In Chapter 2 we referred to the characteristic phases of creative process, assembled from reports of the greatly varying experience of artists, scientists and others. Out of the speculative, free play with possibilities on which all creative work is based, one's attention is caught, sustained, and focused as a kind of personal question; this questioning requires some kind of plan or idea if the original challenge is to be realized. If one could get that plan from a teacher or out of a book, we noted, he would not need to bother with the difficulties, even the pain, of the creative process.

But such a ready-made plan would not embody the special kind of individual seeing and enjoying which has given the question personal importance.

The finding of materials can itself call upon and incorporate individual experience. In the process there may emerge, more or less clearly, a sense of direction or purpose for continuing work on the questions raised by the pleasures of finding. Sensuous enjoyment remains the guide, and personal expression the motivation for the labor of giving form to what one has found.

There are many subtle ways in which different kinds of purposing or motivation can affect aesthetic experience and creative work. Children whose collecting of insects is aimed at winning a prize — even an imagined one — learn that enjoying differences is less efficient than recognizing them, and that, far from "finding materials," one gets things in order to get other things. Thus work and play become the shortest line to somewhere else, and materials are chosen to help one get there.

We know that purposing does not lead necessarily to this kind of blind instrumentalism in working experience. One may "idly" pick something up, turning, twisting, and observing it, and then proceed to "look for" something else which will go with it, interact with it, help it. There is a kind of purpose in such action which is familiar to most of us and, on a different scale, well known to the artist. Such purposes are expressed as personal questions, asked in action, and becoming increasingly focused, urgent, and even obsessive as one seeks to give the right form to "how I see it."

If this kind of purpose is unacceptable to us it is probably because, in drawing a line between work and play, improvisation and discovery have fallen on the side of the ineffectual and unworthy. Probably instructing children for life's errands will always stress, "Go straight there and come straight home." But in spite of this, children still move easily from discovery to statement. To them the sufficient purpose of "finding materials" is set by the rich and wonderful fact of being alive. They take action noting what happens. But whether what happens is product or process is not the key to their satisfaction and learning in aesthetic response and inventive construction.

In this chapter we have been raising questions about what goes on in finding materials, and how such finding enters into aesthetic experience and creative work. The questions raised in this general way need to be made much more personal and immediate by the reader himself if they are to lead to the kind of insights and convictions useful to teachers of children. Especially, these teachers know that aesthetic experience is actively sought by individuals, not doled out in some kind of learners' bread line, however philanthropic. Teachers also know that their best-laid lesson plans serve only as points of departure when real and unpredictable individuals go into action.

The questions at the end of this chapter ask the reader to apply his personal experience, as an individual and as a teacher, to certain processes of finding materials.

The experiments on rubbings which follow in the next chapter are designed to help adults take an inside look at some elementary processes of aesthetic experience and creative venture.

Questions

1. On page 18 are listed some characteristics of stuffs and objects which might affect their usefulness as materials for creative work or play. Try to apply these to different play supplies, equipment, and toys which parents might give to children. If you were constructing a "Materials Rating Scale" to help parents' choices, what are some of the questions you would include?
2. From your own experience or observation, describe an example of each of the four "ways of responding to things" listed on page 19.
3. Discuss the difference between quick dismissal and tentative rejection or putting aside. Cite examples from your experience in (a) working with physical materials, (b) considering ideas or solutions to a problem, or (c) meeting strangers.
4. The discussion of where materials are found, on page 20, compares "extended" finding in an open setting with "intensified" finding within a preselected range. Describe examples of both kinds of finding, perhaps in connection with a field trip, travel, a walk, or a visit, and compare their importance to you, your feeling about them, etc.
5. To what extent do you think the supervision and supply of a classroom materials collection should be the responsibility of the teacher? Of the children? Of parents and others? (Specify school setting, grade level, etc.)

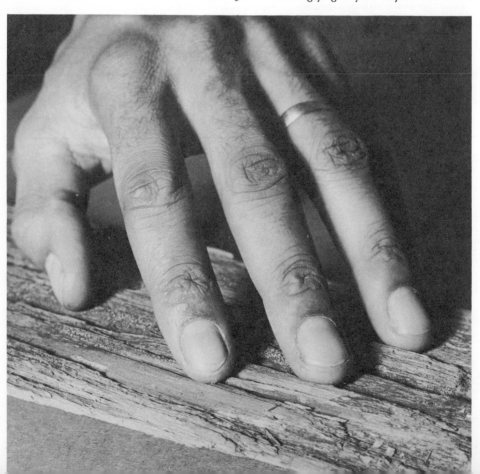

4

Experiments with Found
Materials: Rubbings

In years of "looking around," we have stored away a wealth of sensory impressions, more or less lively. To recall most of these would probably mean to see them, but such mental pictures depend on more than vision.

No doubt we once had to be told that good boys and girls "do not touch." Learning by running our hands over the surfaces of things was gradually put aside until in adulthood we assent to burying the tactile qualities of wood grain, raw linen, ground cork, or marble chips in miles of mass produced plastic. If our fingers should want to touch the resulting stuff, their prints could at least be easily removed.

However, there is still a great variety of roughened, bumpy, fluted, fibrous, scarred, machined, veined, and otherwise interesting tactile surfaces to be discovered and enjoyed by our hands if we look around for them. Of course, looking which is done with the eyes alone might be misled by colors, by varying depths of relief and

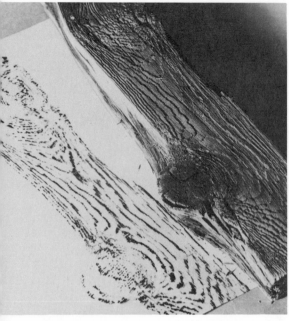

4   *The rippling pattern of wood growth.*

other (temporarily) irrelevant factors. The finger tips can "read" the surface variation better but only when they are in motion. The gaps or incisions or valleys which are cut down into an established surface will feel quite different from ridges, bumps, and mountains rising above a base surface. The sensory effect of meeting such surface variations is not unlike that of hearing percussion.

5   *Skill in holding and rubbing develops*
      naturally.

Experiment 1:

Rubbings

Within the broad range of found, tactile possibilities, literally at our fingertips, we can select a smaller group for the patterns they would make in rubbings. The process of making a rubbing, sometimes called *frottage,* is familiar to us if we have ever tried scribbling on a sheet of paper held over a penny, capturing Abe Lincoln and the accompanying words in precise detail.

Finding the Materials

For our present purposes of hunting and finding we shall use the side of unwrapped wax crayons and work on sheets of fairly thin, soft paper. The cheapest grade of smooth newsprint works well, as do onion skin sheets from a secretarial supply. Pieces of "expression crayons," which come without covering, are especially suitable, but almost any kind will do. Having a variety of light and dark colors will probably help.

Using many sheets of paper, try out the surfaces in your room—the floor, the wood work, grilles, radiators, furniture, whatever looks and feels likely—and then move on out to other rooms, the door, the yard, the street, or wherever the hunt leads you. Such wide-ranging exploration may be extended and enriched greatly by the companionship of fellow hunters.

As you work you will become more skillful at holding the paper stretched over the surface you are recording and at rubbing the crayon to capture the relief configurations which interest you. If the paper slips and you get a double image, it may suggest possibilities of extended repeating, regularly or irregularly spaced.

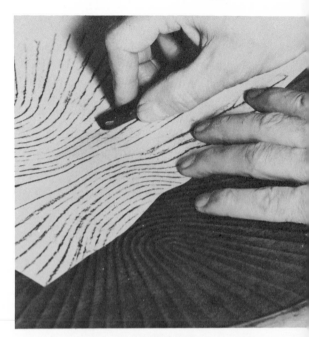

6   *Wave-like curves from a chair seat.*

Perhaps only part of the pattern made by a surface will work better than all of it. Try making some parts appear very clearly and letting other parts fade out. If you find the crayon makes extra marks outside the impression you wish to record, don't let it bother you too much. A shorter crayon with rounded ends may help.* What you are looking for in every case is something you like, something lovely or intriguing, something special even in its strange or stubborn character.

This looking for something you like needs to be relaxed and easy-going. "Liking" is sometimes dependent on recognizing images, as when we see dogs, birds, or faces in a pattern. This is natural after life-long answering to "What is that?" And since the requirement is that *you* like it, your own mixture of reasons, based on your own mixture of experiences, is your guide. However, the more you can notice *how* it is, along with what it resembles or what it came from, the better your aesthetic experience. Thus the clean, swinging arcs from a garbage can lid are visually different from the fluid curves

7   *Letter patterns swing in arcs.*

---

*Sometimes cutting out the rubbings (of ferns or leaves, for example) and mounting them on colored paper makes them show more clearly.

of the pressed wood chair seat or the irregular blockiness from the alligator handbag. What you are working with here are clean, swinging arcs, fluid curves, and irregular blockiness. *These are your found materials,* not the paper and crayon, nor the garbage can, chair or handbag, which serve as supplies, equipment and sources. This is because we are involved in exploring aesthetic experience and creative working, rather than simply "making rubbings."

It is true that the production of clear rubbings to record the surfaces of individual things can be a useful activity in its own right. For example, a recent museum exhibition featured beautifully made rubbings of early American grave stones. Again, in a third grade, the children's rubbings became a wall display of individually discovered surface patterns titled "From Our Room to the Front Gate."

Rubbed recordings can no doubt capture aesthetic qualities found in certain objects and offer them as materials for the viewer's aesthetic enjoyment—of the stair tread, the cement walk, Billy's sneaker, and so on. However, these uses are primarily statements of how *it* is—the carved grave stone, for example, or Billy's sneaker. Of course, such object-centered rubbings may also say something about the recorder's finding and selecting; but for purposes of studying aesthetic experience and creative working it would be better to consider the hunting process described so far as preparatory play and to think of the personal discoveries of special qualities in surface pattern as one's *found materials.*

Experiment 2:

Creating a Composition

Next, therefore, comes the "using" of the materials which have been found. This means, while continuing the process of selection which began when you first noticed possibilities, you now select which of your visual materials might work well in relationship, and find how they might do that best. The point, of course, is not to see how many can be combined and mixed together, for it may be that variations of just one material will do what you want.

In composing, the best plan is to *go with* the special, visual character you have found in your materials—for example, a tawny, ragged brusqueness, or a long, gentle, wavy grace, or a strong, fast-curving sweep, or a boxy, building-like pile-up. To "go with" means to take action in response to something you like or identify with, something whose way of behaving, in this case visually, fits your tastes and experience. In short, you should continue play with your materials to bring out what they have. See how these qualities can interact to develop a kind of satisfying, easy wholeness.

A secondary kind of experimenting to increase control and variation of techniques will provide greater freedom for such visual play with material. To make a part stand out among the relationships of a composition may call for more contrast in color, in dark and light, or in definition. It may also call for subordination or simplification of other, "background" parts. Too much and too many contrasts and stand-out features are usually self-defeating. In fact, a beginning wish to "do something different" often confuses first efforts, until relaxing and really "liking it" can give surer direction to choices.

It may be a visual theme rather than a "part" which will take the lead in your composing, and you may find yourself stating it, supporting, restating, or echoing it—as well as departing from or opposing it—through the developing shapes, spaces, directions and networks of pattern and colors.

The aesthetic choices made to achieve generalized standards of decorative acceptability ("good taste") are different from those made to give effective form to the thinking/feeling ("I like") experience of an individual. Outside help to the former might be hindrance to the latter. Most teachers would agree that advice to the creator is best offered in the form of questions. But where the right to find one's own answers has not been established, questions may seem to be only different forms of authoritarian commands. This is a subtle but essential distinction and another reason why a teacher needs to ask himself what kinds of questioning help his own creative work.

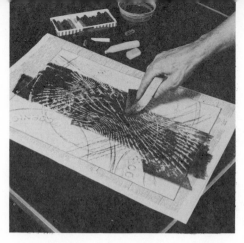

8   *Sponging over the crayon wax composition of three rubbing "materials" — arcs, waves, and straight lines.*

9   *Man-made and natural surfaces.*

10   *Watching the water paint run off the wax.*

Experiment 3:

Batik

The wax crayons make possible a batik or "wax resist" variation in the process of composing your rubbings. This is done by sponging ink, dye, or thinned water color or poster paints over the rubbed pattern of colored wax. If this ink or water color wash is black or a dark color it will produce a dramatic reversal of the former order of light-dark contrasts. For example, a yellow pattern formerly quite faint against the white paper will now stand out like night-time neon lights. This can be carried further by using in the rubbing process a piece of ordinary colorless paraffin or candle. Its visible marks will loom out even more vividly than those of the crayons after dark water color is applied to the sheet. Again some experimenting will be needed to arrive at a heavy enough wax deposit to repel or resist the water color.

11   *Sponging can become the main interest.*

Extension or Distraction?

One should ask himself whether adding such a technical extension as water color batik to the process of composing the found materials of rubbings will strengthen or confuse the experience. For example, one can imagine a child making a rubbing over a classroom radiator shield and beginning to find a pattern he liked. Suddenly he hears his friend exclaim, "Boy, look at that!" and sees the spectacular effect of batik. It might be hard to continue his work with the radiator shield.

The batik variation was included here partly to add contrast to the faint whispering of crayons alone. But more importantly, such a variation *may* help to involve us more deeply in the process of composing with our rubbing discoveries.

Whether a suggested extension in technique will intensify our creative work or turn it into superficial busy-work depends on the kinds of working questions we are led to ask ourselves. The depth of our involvement in a central question is, of course, what makes other questions comparatively less central at a given moment, but it also insures that when added alternatives are brought into focus they will not be distracting. Thus the boy rubbing the radiator shield might have responded to the batik suggestion, "Wait till you see what *I'm* getting!"

Such focusing is individual and changing. It may also be strongly influenced by social pressures. In the value pattern of our school culture it would probably be "off-beat" to concentrate on aesthetic qualities of rubbings rather than on identification of their sources, or to stress creative process rather than the things produced.

"Something to Show"?

As teachers we are influenced by the openness of our children so that we may give only partial loyalty to utilitarian standards. But few of us could experiment wholeheartedly in art without some kind of "take-home" products—something to show for the work. Of course, the developing product of our work is important to us in every stage as a reflection of our recorded choices, and often we can continue to learn from later study of our work. But in making end-products the aim of creative work, the danger—both individual and professional—lies in subordinating responsibility for the quality of our own involvement in favor of the heady satisfaction of hearing others' praise. This is a common way of subverting children's aesthetic and creative development.

Practical advice for handling the products of our own aesthetic experiments might be to keep them accessible for whatever study we, or our close friends, wished to give them, but not to ask our end-products to go out into the world to lead a life of their own. For example, putting up our work on "our own" bulletin board, to be seen only by those who know us and how we did it, is very different from exhibiting it out in a "front hall," where it will be viewed simply as a product, cut off from the uniqueness of our working process. Sometimes comparing our work with our own earlier work—the only valid comparison—will help us answer, "What next?"

One advantage of rubbings for our experimenting is the fact that we are not likely to judge our products in comparison with those of master artists in the medium, since artists' use of comparable surface qualities of objects for inventive composition is usually confined to print making. However, study of the professional rubbings in museums by artist-archaeologists will reveal techniques for capturing subtle differences, such as by dry-ink pouncing, by rolling printer's ink sparingly over masked surfaces with soft brayers, and by using rice papers, silks, and "unwoven cloth." Some of these rubbings of prehistoric wall carvings or of ancient gravestones are very beautiful.

Even though we may find few rubbings by professional artists, our work in developing compositions will provide us with new pleasure in the world around us. In finding the materials of the rubbings, we are also finding unsuspected tactile differences. But in developing organized, expressive pattern images, using color, spacing, dark and light, we were studying relationships and saying something by composing. This experience can lead us into more responsible observation of visual relationships in the environment, such as juxtaposition of plant tracery against wall textures, of fire escapes and television aerials against smoke and clouds, and other examples of spatial transparency and overlay.

Questions

Work with rubbings could involve the individual in aesthetic development and creative work *or* it could instead turn toward superficial busy-work and impersonal product-making. What are the differences in the kinds of questioning which would lead us in one or the other of these directions? For example, in the "finding" part of the work on rubbings, try to imagine what questions might direct us toward involvement and what ones toward busy-work in:

preliminary planning

getting started

setting up a working plan

solving technical problems

seeing and evaluating differences found in the materials.

And after the finding, what questions might lead us to opposite kinds of "using" of the materials we found in:

selecting and organizing our materials

working out and evaluating organized visual statements

looking ahead to extension and follow-up.

5

Making Prints with Found Objects

The processes of finding embossed or incised surfaces for rubbings and using their patterns as materials for inventive visual statements lead quite naturally into the much more variable and controllable processes of print making. This is a field of expression to which many artists have devoted their lives and through which they are presenting some of the most compelling images of the present day.

Print making is also one of the most rewarding fields for the student and the collector. There is a wealth of technical knowledge about print making, in its many branches as an art form and in its complex applications in commercial printing and mass production. Whether one's interest is in the enjoyment of others' prints or in learning to make one's own, there is a wide range of books and other resources ready for investigation. In school art programs, for example, print making, once confined to linoleum blocks for older children, has branched out in many directions and now offers important aesthetic learning experience for young and old.

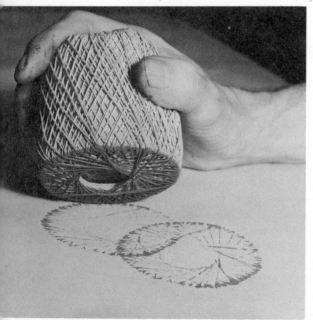

12   *Stamp printing with found objects and inking pads.*

13   *Trying out a printer.*

Experiment 4:

Print Making

For our present purposes we shall confine ourselves to print making with found objects. As in all kinds of printing there are three parts to the working process:

1. Preparing the "printer" (in this case finding and trying out imprinting, relief surfaces).

2. Inking the printer (applying colored paint or ink to those surfaces).

3. Imprinting the inked image on paper or some other surface.

The process of finding relief surfaces for imprinters or "printers" is similar to that described for rubbings. However, printers usually need to be portable so that they can be picked up, inked, and placed where they are to be printed.

The finding process is again not complete until the surfaces have been tried out and expressive visual possibilities revealed. This involves experimenting with inking or "charging" the printer with the pigmented medium which is to be transferred to a surface, such as paper or cloth. Precise control of this inking process is an important part of the printmaker's work, and the many methods he uses yield a wide range of results.

For our experiments with found object printers, the simple inking methods used by children will probably be adequate. For repeated inking of printers, the kind of inking pad which children use for stamp printing with cut pieces of potato will be satisfactory. These pads are made of pieces of heavy, absorbent rags, preferably with a nap, such as cotton flannel or terry cloth. After wetting and wringing out these cloths, work tempera paint into them with a brush, mixing whatever special colors you wish. These flat, folded pads, charged but not puddled with color, are spread out on some kind of flat plate. The found-object printer, such as the rough-sawn end of a piece of wood, the mouth of a jar, the edge of a piece of cardboard, or the end of a seed pod, is first pressed down on the pad to receive its charge of color, and then onto the sheet of paper. For taking trial impressions paper towels are satisfactory. Each impression requires re-inking of the printer. The charge of ink or paint should be light enough to reveal the precise outline and surface structure which one likes in the found-object printer.

If a special color is desired for only a few impressions, it may be patted onto the surface of the printer with a paint brush, to avoid preparing one of the inking pads.

Some printers offer special problems of inking and printing. A button or shell, for example, may need a thread or wire-loop handle so that it can be printed and picked up without unwanted finger prints. On the other hand, a piece of coarse netting or a loop of string, after being charged with color, may be laid in place and covered with paper so the impression can be rubbed on to the printing sheet. For these and other flat, thin printers a clothes wringer or roller-type printing press will apply more pressure and produce a clearer imprint.

Some kinds of larger relief surfaces do not lend themselves to inking with stamp pads or paint brushes. For these a brayer or paint roller, and block printing inks give greater control of inking and more definition in the impression. Unless you are prepared to clean up with turpentine, use water soluble printing inks, first rolling them out on a piece of glass or flooring tile and then applying them to the surface of the printer.

In making the impression of the printer on paper, the principle to remember is that the pressure required depends on the extent of the printing area. Thus it takes many times more pressure to print a board or a linoleum block than to print the end of a pencil eraser. To print large surfaces lay the paper over the inked printer and rub it with the bowl of a spoon. Of course, some found printers, like a sponge or a crumpled tissue, require a light touch rather than strong pressure. Because found-object printers often have more up-and-down surface variations than do carved printing plates, it may be found helpful to pad the table top on which the prints are made.

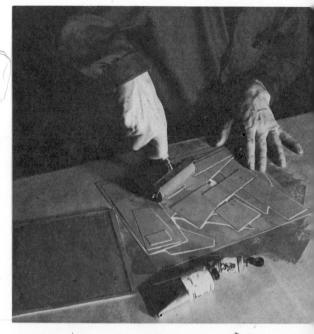

14   *Using brayer and printer's ink in cardboard printing.*
15   *Pulling a print with a clothes wringer.*

Almost any papers are suited to this process, provided they are soft enough to receive the ink with the limited pressure which can be applied to many of the found printers. The sheets of tissue paper used by children for printing gift wraps are satisfactory, as are heavier, soft-finished papers.

While the technical directions for print making which have been included here should be adequate for beginning experimental print making with found objects, these first efforts will doubtless lead to further investigations and require additional technical information.* As with rubbings, finding and trying out printers will produce a variety of expressive elements or patterns. This "cast of characters" will be the found materials which can then be used in developing print compositions. The processes are similar to those in rubbing, but color, placement, and definition can be controlled more completely in printing.

Experimenting with print making can bring special insights to our study of the creative process. Although rubbings and prints have much in common, they differ in one characteristic: the technical, manipulative skills required for the rubbing medium tend to be much less demanding than are those for printing. As a result, the creative process experienced in making rubbings is likely to emphasize exploratory play and discovery of form more than the working out or realization of the form. The technical problems involved in print making, on the other hand, are likely to focus the attention on problem-solving aspects of working out the printing process, especially where a printed composition is produced more than once.

Of course, work in either medium can be varied tremendously, offering different kinds of individual satisfaction as creative work while still focusing on the "pay-off" part, the personal statement or composition. Because this can be so rich in meaning to the experimenter, it is essential that he become involved with the processes of aesthetic (not just technical) elaboration, adjustment, and variation which printing media can offer with special clarity.

Experimenting in print making, more than with rubbings, can add to the study and enjoyment of many kinds of prints being produced by professional print makers. While some contemporary work uses mixed methods, including found object printing, most prints will be found to carry on the more traditional and technically demanding methods of print making, by which small "editions" of prints are produced.

---

*See Bibliography, pp. 201.

Exhibits of good art prints are increasingly accessible to most people these days to study, enjoy, and even to purchase. The type of print—etching, drypoint, lithograph, wood cut, collotype, serigraph, or other—is interesting to know, but less important than looking at it and letting it invite you to continue studying it; for this and the signature's witness of the artist's hand, it is satisfying to have good prints in one's home.

Even more than with rubbings, the experience of composing prints with found objects will draw upon and clarify observations of one's environment, especially the relationships of simultaneous and overlapping and otherwise coexistent *visual* "events." In a city night, for example, one *hears* passing trucks rising and falling over the steady murmur of an electric motor, then sharp words, rising laughter, the motor again, and so on; it is not difficult to find the qualities of similar relationships in one's days and years. Such observing may seem far away from the visual composing of print making, but it is familiar content to those who have themselves moved into the work of creating prints.

Questions

1. With what different kinds of print making have you experimented? Describe the difference in emphasis and control required in the working process of each method. How do they differ in the learning satisfactions they would offer young children? Older children?

2. Cite a specific example of satisfaction which work in print making can offer the amateur. Discuss how this aesthetic "pay-off" may be enriched by focusing on limited technical means, and how by extending technical alternatives.

3. The printing experiments described in this chapter suggest over-printing, perhaps with several printers and colors of ink, rather than concentrating on a single impression in one color. This way of seeing images in relationship (different layers or levels at the same time) is a growing interest in the arts. Cite examples of the use of this "simultaneity" in architecture, drama, sculpture, music, or other arts fields.

16   *Making prints increases our response to overlay and transparency.*

6

Imprinting Relief Surfaces
with Found Objects

The found materials used in rubbing and printing are the patterns of top surfaces of things, first spotted by the eyes, perhaps, but really discovered by the fingers. Both the rubbings and the prints may have reached more deeply than the topmost surfaces; but the outermost planes were most clearly perceived and others less so, until deeply recessed surfaces of objects were entirely omitted.

The sculptor carving into a block of stone works in a similar way, often retaining outside planes from the block's original face as he works back into the volume of the block. Study of the design of frontal planes of reliefs, as in the carved metopes of the frieze which crowns the Parthenon, reveals that by themselves these front planes would make satisfying visual statements, even without most of the carved modeling of bulls and athletes or their "flat" stone background. Similar front-plane clarity appears as a strong element in the temple carvings of India.

Experiment 5:

Imprinting Clay

Work with the found materials of surfaces may lead to a quite different kind of experiment which captures not only the outer planes of the touched surfaces, but also the full three-dimensional form of relief. And since our purpose is to explore aesthetic/creative processes, we go beyond our usual "What is it?" kind of touching-feeling to savor such differences as round and flat, smooth and rough, delicate and coarse, sharp and dull, concave and convex, repeated and single, regular and irregular. No doubt we shall find many of these relief qualities in objects we can pick up and move, as well as in walls, trees, and stoves.

Once more our selecting and finding must set aside, tentatively, visual attributes of color, dark and light, internal structure, and nominal identity; in addition, to try out and then to use the selected relief aspect of objects, we turn to a process which will help us clarify and objectify that aesthetic aspect in manageable form.

In this process, the found relief surface is pressed into a small slab of soft clay to make a three-dimensional imprint. Many attempts may be made and the clay surface scraped flat again. Sometimes a single object, like a shell or a rough piece of wood, shows its qualities in many different ways, making it likely material for repetition and variation. Different shape categories or families of impressions, not of imprinters, will appear as all-over patterns, rounded hollow cups, or box-like planes and ridges; all of these will be seen in the geometric regularity of the machine-made objects or in the growth variations of natural ones. Rippling, staccato delicacy, stormy crashes, and bumbling informality will appear. In order that this trying-out process may lead to finding materials, a kind of attentive playfulness is required, bent more on pleasure in what is happening than on getting a job done.

Out of kinds of "I like that," experienced in this preliminary play, there will begin to develop an arrange-

17   *Selecting imprints to compose a clay slab relief.*

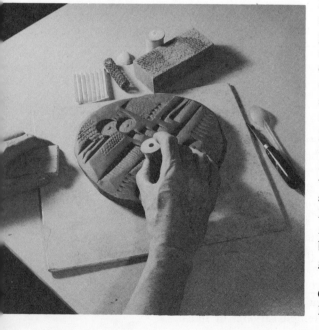

ment or composition which will incorporate, bring out, elaborate, or say what and how it is that "I like" in clay slab relief. This phase of the work is, again, the "payoff area," where the individual finds his main satisfaction.

It Should Not Be Hurried

As in the rubbing or printing experiments, the first clear impression of an object in the clay surface is sometimes so effective and so satisfying by itself that one may wish only to record its uniqueness. In this case the discovered imprint would become the end product. But it is usually more rewarding to use it as a found material, to be varied, repeated, and associated with other imprints in composing a rich relief surface. Thus, by working with the visual qualities of the materials, a new whole may be created, more exciting than any of its original parts. The characteristics of the imprint materials are played informally back and forth within the clay surface, using emphasis, overlapping, reappearing, continuing, subordinating, and other helpful kinds of interaction. Perhaps a feeling of "place" such as an imaginary landscape or cityscape may develop. In any case, it is better to continue than to worry about spoiling one's efforts.

18   *Making a plaster cast of the imprinted relief.*

As the composition becomes livelier it may also become too complicated; but then, by selecting and reinforcing what seem to be the most evocative characteristics, a new, simplified order can be achieved. The simplicity won by working on through such stages of disorder will almost surely be more individually expressive than the safe but empty tastefulness with which most of us begin. Although both are simple, they are entirely different; this difference is an important part of creative process.

Experiment 6:

Casting in Plaster

Technically, the imprint of forms into the clay becomes a precise negative record of them. A close-up photograph of the imprinted clay composition, taken with side lighting, will record its relief permanently. Or using the imprinted clay as a mold, one may pour in

19   *Variations of planes and textures in imprinted sand.*

20   *Casting converts negative imprints into positive relief.*

plaster of paris to make a cast, making the forms positive again and making the imprinted composition permanent. To do this, add a clay wall to the slab by rolling out a clay coil and flattening it into a strap long enough to go around the slab and high enough to project about three quarters of an inch above its surface.

If you have never worked with plaster, follow these directions. Plaster of paris or quick-setting plaster is available at lumber, hardware, or paint dealers. Be sure to work away from the sink and provide a pail or other water container for cleanup to avoid blocking the drains with plaster. Wear rubber gloves or use vaseline to protect your hands. Into a pan of water (as much as your mold will require) slowly sprinkle the dry plaster until it stands above the water's surface in small islands. When these islands are wet, stir the plaster thoroughly and pour it into the mold. Try to joggle the table or the board on which the mold sits so that locked-in air bubbles can float to the surface of the plaster. A wire or paper clip set in the wet plaster will provide for later hanging.

The plaster will set in about a half hour, when it will become warm. Remove the clay wall and the clay slab and wash the plaster cast, if you wish. If specks of plaster are removed from the clay it may be stored for further use. In cleaning up, remember to keep plaster away from the sink.

Experiment 7:
Adding Color to Relief

Since your imprinted clay and plaster do not capture the colors of the objects used, your relief is composed of the three-dimensional differences only. Study these forms in their new state and relationship to see whether and how the effect of the relief composition could be enhanced by adding color. Using poster paints or water colors with small brushes, try painting parts of your plaster cast, perhaps continuing until you have applied color to all of it. Whether you will hold to a narrow range or family of colors or try strong contrasts will depend on the character of the relief.

Observe the effect of the new color factor on the three-dimensional form. Although placing it in a strong cross light may restore the form somewhat, you may find that the color has overpowered some of the relief surfaces and forms. In this case, try washing off some of the paint under a faucet until the balance of form and color staining seems right to you.

Experiment 8:

Imprinting Sand

Children who have made these imprinted reliefs have called them "fossils" because of their captured tracks or traces of objects. One of the most exciting three-dimensional working experiences is to imprint a surface of damp beach sand with larger forms, such as sticks, boards, bottles, or shells. Such a relief can also be cast in plaster, mixed thin and poured on gently. Compared to clay the sand omits the subtler surface textures of objects, having a beautiful texture of its own; but it focuses the attention on the sculptural interplay of larger planes and volumes within a relief structure.

21 *Combining modeled form with imprints.*

One must now ask himself whether our well-established habits of purposeful production are so stratified by how-to directions, such as those above for plaster casting, that they overshadow or cut short the exploratory finding of materials and the creative development of a relief composition.

We might feel such pressure for many reasons. If time is limited, and it usually is, then the "indefinite" part (the playful, enjoying, trying, changing, responding, and experimenting part which constitutes the aesthetic and creative experience) is likely to be abandoned in order to get on with the "definite" part, the careful steps of the product making, which seems to guarantee acceptability of one's work.

Most of us bring a degree of self-doubt or skepticism to creative work in a social situation. If there is to be a product it should be creditable and praiseworthy, and any finding of materials should be aimed at this goal. Thus we may hope that securing some extraordinary object to work with, a starfish, for example, will add so much interest to the product that our lack of design experience will not be noticed. A little marginal watching and listening may show what does or does not merit official approval and what the experts in the group are doing.

Product-centered work also harbors a point of vulnerability for the teacher, who is the authority. "Just watch me," and "Just do as I say," really belong with directions for clay wall building and plaster mixing. And after all, what *is* a teacher, and how does he know he is teaching if he is not "telling"?

One cure for such anxieties might be to make the indefinite part of aesthetic-creative work more definite, and indeed, that is a purpose of our experiments. But, try as we may, we cannot avoid threats to our self-esteem or doubts of our individual integrity in the risky business of living independently. Rather than retire into self-defense, we can engage ourselves more generously in ventures which may yield the satisfaction of affirming, "The way I did that feels right!" When used for such continued learning, end products can be an important part of a creative working process. It is pleasant to come upon one of your "fossils" half hidden among the plants in your garden and to recall its venturesome construction.

Some will protest the impersonal aspects of such a process as taking a rough piece of wood, pressing it down at an angle into clay, then moving it along and pressing it more deeply, then again, still more deeply—always watching those increasing depths of shadow and the play of soft and sharp within them. If a product results, some would question whether the person or the piece of wood created it.

22   *Working into three-dimensional form with imprints.*

Certainly working with found materials is a kind of interaction, and passive or aggressive roles will vary. The guiding direction should be to "get *with* it!", which means not only concentrating on efficient problem solving but also involving one's self and one's experience. This in turn means taking the personal responsibility of saying, "I am and I see", and also, "I like and I say."

Working with relief surfaces leads to an enriched way of seeing one's environment. As in rubbings and prints, the depth variations of surface in "fossils" are separated from other attributes such as color. Having refreshed one's awareness of this surface variation through touching, taking, and using, one can respond to it as one of the many factors at work in a sensory situation. In their relief of surface, weatherbeaten wood, bark, eroded soil, or wind-swept sand present part of their history. The shift from the fluted continuity of the column to the playful spread of its capital shows in outer relief what is being done inside. In contrast, many houses, both natural and man-made, smooth the inner pouch by keeping the bony structure outside, again expressing the inner function through outer surfaces.

Working on "fossils" concentrates our eyes, hands, and imagination on the varied topography of our surroundings. It also reveals the transcendent power in the eyes, hands, and imagination of the great architect and sculptor. With our amateur making (more than with our products) we can learn to share their life-long making through their products. We can see, for example, the contained power of the Assyrian lion kings within the carving of their dense stone surfaces. The rich muscularity of Louis Sullivan's buildings is revealed and celebrated by his relief inventions; and more recently, Constantin Nivola has given full sculptural play to his relief walls.

Questions

1. Rubbings, prints, and imprinted reliefs capture different aspects of the surfaces of objects. Try to describe these differences in character or feeling, focusing on the special qualities of each medium.

2. In Experiments five and six you proceeded from a positive object, to a negative track or mold, to a positive cast. What differences did you observe in your working experience in these changing processes? Where did you find most interest or satisfaction?

3. Experiment seven, adding color to relief, touches on a question of great importance: how do differences in color affect three-dimensionality? Cite examples of multi-colored relief surfaces in nature in which color differences are subtle or outstanding, and compare them with monochromatic relief.

   Look for examples of man-made relief, with and without color differentiation, as in buildings, fabrics, etc., and also in sculpture with or without polychrome.

23 *Seeing through the overlapping folds of a "light sifter."*

7

Found Materials as
Tracery and Transparency

We have seen how touching helps us find visual materials for aesthetic experience and imaginative construction. In addition, one's finding can involve the larger muscles in moving, lifting, reaching, and pushing in the three dimensional world of sculpture and architecture. These working processes are examined in Chapters 12, 17, and 18.

Some kinds of finding, enjoying, and working with materials seem to be almost entirely visual, or at least they begin that way. One such family of visual experiences comes from looking up, for example, from one's bed or chair, from the city street or the woodland path, and seeing the light filtering through the tracery and silhouettes of "light sifters." The gradations through overlapping folds of curtains, the angular slits and slashes of light through fire escapes, grids and gratings, and the endless play of pattern through trees, grasses, clouds, and smoke all remind the hunter for materials to "hold it up to the light."

Working with Tracery and Silhouettes

To see through means to move through, at least in eye focus and convergence, but the space dividers thus seen can also be captured in projected tracery, as in the shadows of twigs and branches cast by the sun on wall or ground. Such a pattern network, formed by more or less opaque silhouettes of objects in space, can be studied in many ways, beginning with looking through stuffs and objects toward the light.

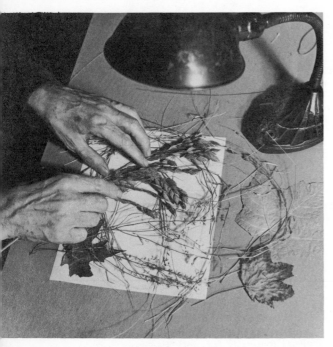

24   *A photogram may be planned outside the darkroom and later transferred to photoprint paper.*

Experiment 9:
Recording on Photo-Sensitive Surfaces

Finding can lead to selecting and recording with a camera; this is one of the best ways to relate oneself to the visual environment in ventures of looking and seeing. With suitable equipment one can photograph arrangements of light-sifters or their projected shadows. Photosensitive surfaces can also be used without a camera to record transparency, tracery, and silhouettes in photograms. Both blue prints and photograms offer much freedom of choice in the selection, association, and arrangement of small light-sifters.

Blueprint methods used in schools require that the pattern-producing object be held flat against the paper in exposure to light. Less sensitive than photographic printing paper, blueprinting paper can be used in subdued light, next exposed to the sun or a lamp, and then fixed and washed. For more complete instructions, consult the Appendix, p. 189.

Making photograms requires a darkroom and the equipment for photographic printing. Photograms, having a greater range of dark/light sensitivity than blueprints, can record delicate differences in opacity and definition. Again, see the Appendix, p. 189, for further working directions.

A good way to find and to work with light-sifters and see-throughs is to place them between pieces of glass or other transparent sheets. Sometimes a suitable window can be found for such a see-through sandwich. A transparent panel in a room divider, backed by a light source, can also provide a setup for studying the tracery of many kinds of pattern makers, such as grasses, ferns, lace, nets, or bits of photographic negatives and transparencies.

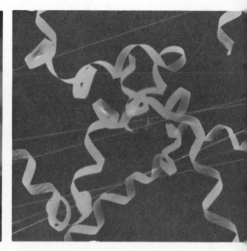

25 *One light exposure will record a photogram arrangement, or a series will allow overlays of shadows.*

Experiment 10:

Lantern Slides

The great advantage of enlargement makes working with the slide projector an especially exciting way to compose with light-filtering materials. The larger 3¼″ by 4″ lantern slide is easier to work with, but 2″ by 2″ slides can also receive a great range of tiny, delicate fibers, nets, filaments, granules, and bits of opaque and translucent substances; they can become materials for different, often dramatic, projected images of arranged dark/light pattern. To this tracery of opaque found materials can be added the brilliance of projected color, for such glass sandwiches can also receive pieces and overlays of colored cellophane, theatrical gelatines, colored inks, and varied films of such translucent materials as rubber cement. Because of the enlargement and because things are often less translucent than expected, these surprises will bring new responses—continuing, not ending the interaction. Hinging two glass slide covers together by taping along one edge will allow reopening for changing and adjustment of the materials.

26 *Lantern slides can project delicate tracery and brilliant color.*

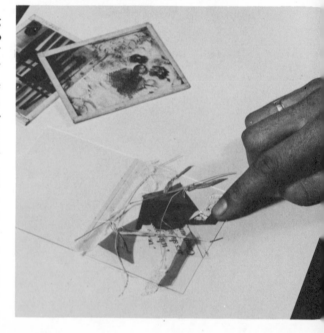

27   *Crayon scrapings are added to an arrangement of light sifters . .* 28   *. . . and melted between layers of wax paper.*

Experiment 11:

Laminated Wax Transparencies

Another common way to work with found light sifters, without cameras, dark rooms, or projectors, is to iron them between layers of waxed paper, again using only light sifters which have little thickness, such as fine threads, laces, nets, or insect-eaten leaves. Adding a small amount of scraped paraffin to the wax already in the waxed paper permits sealing the materials between layers with a warm iron. Scrapings of colored wax crayons can be placed so they will add washlike transparent color when melted, and cut pieces of cellophane or theatrical gelatine will add color which remains defined in shape. Because the heat of the iron results in some unforeseen, uncontrolled changes, especially in the melting wax, some parts of the laminated transparency will be more satisfying than others; thus, cutting out or mask-

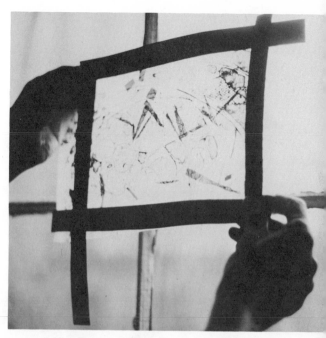

Inspecting the transparency against the light . . . .   *. . . and masking the selected section.*

ing certain areas will suitably continue the finding process. Mounted on a window or against white paper, these
transparencies will allow continued study and enjoyment.

Craft supply companies offer a variety of plastic sheets, solvents, and cements
for producing more permanent laminated transparencies. However, these are not
necessary for our purpose of visual enjoyment.

We often see traceries in our three-dimensional environment, and their shifting
relationships are visually exciting. Such observation will suggest further experiments with two or more layers of laminated transparencies moving at different
speeds across a light source. The extent of the possibilities may be seen in some of
the optical constructions and kinetic sculptures of contemporary artists.

It is easy to change one's goal from finding and composing with see-through
materials to turning out transparencies which others will want because they are
"interesting" or "effective." In order to keep the main emphasis on individual,
aesthetic experience, it sometimes helps to keep right on working beyond the "finished product" stage, replacing the fear of spoiled work with a drive to see where
the work will lead.

31 *Staves swing across sand in linear thrusts — texture, color, spacing.*

8

Collage from Found Materials

Aesthetic response to environmental objects is usually overshadowed by the complex associations which come from a lifetime of reading labels. Names, directions for use, lists of ingredients, and appropriate warnings are all information which we need to know. The label for a sunset or a rose reads, "good for aesthetic response"; but when prior associations with an object make personal sensory enjoyment a less likely part of observing it clearly, focusing on one specific aesthetic factor facilitates seeing and finding. For this reason working on such a selective activity as rubbings was presented as better than work with collage for a first approach to aesthetic refreshment. The difference is somewhat like listening to a friend's voice on a tape recording instead of face-to-face.

Collage, which means pasting, suggests fastening flat materials to a two-dimensional surface. In collage, the visual qualities of each material are retained and the action—which quality says what and how it says it—is controlled by the composing artist. For example, a cedar shingle might offer flatness, a ridged linearity, a tubular dryness, and a light, silvery sheen with undertones of yellow/orange and dark green.

If it were set next to a hank of natural wool or a piece of blue glass, different qualities would emerge, thus releasing new response.

The finding of a collage material thus becomes response to an aesthetic character, to a perceived ordering of the several qualities and possibilities which are seen in a stuff or an object. Which qualities appear dominant varies from person to person and from situation to situation. Sometimes the whiteness of cotton takes precedence over its softness, or the linearity of movie film over its transparency. The challenge lies in discovering and working with the possibilities of a material rather than judging under which classification it should be filed.*

In collage, the found materials are freely played with as interacting factors of experience. In answering the collage questions, "Which materials, how much, where?" one is also giving his own response to "What goes with what?" This is similar to deciding whether a coarsely knitted white wool sweater goes with the sheen of one's blonde hair or whether a green corduroy pillow brings out or sets off a room's color setting; however, the working process implied by "goes with" can range all the way from mere acceptance of the current decrees of commercial taste makers, to the personally found relationships (not things) which strike one as being just right. The advantage of composing a collage, compared to planning one's clothing or room, is that one can allow oneself to "go with" the putting together of perceived materials in a freely expressive, even lyrical, statement unencumbered by secondary functions or ulterior purposes.

Collage began as an adjunct or extension of painting; this remains its important direction in aesthetic expression. Adaptations of the selecting-arranging-pasting process have opened up many possibilities, not always understood, for children's learning. To simplify aesthetic choices and the technical problems of cutting and fastening, collage materials for young children are usually limited to papers of different colors and textures. Because anyone will find this a helpful way to study color interplay, experiments with colored paper collage are presented in Chapter 15, which concentrates on color. Now we shall investigate the possibilities of working in collage with less restricted materials.

Experiment 12:

Found Materials Collage

Probably the most interesting way to work with collage is to draw upon any or all kinds of found materials which would offer interesting visual qualities for an arrangement on a flat surface. The working process needs to be a continuation of the finding of the materials. Since this finding has been a *response* to certain visual qualities, the materials are already old friends. What is new

---

*See Appendix: "How to Organize and Use Found Materials in School Art Activities," p. 177.

32   *Torn paper collage.*

is how they behave with other old friends under adjusted circumstances such as background and spacing, and how the whole visual arrangement works out.

Begin work by concentrating on your materials, forgetting about background papers or boards until later. Select something which, as it lies on the table before you, you find visually interesting. It will have some special character of its own, perhaps texture or color, or a combination of such qualities. It may be small or large, textured or linear, transparent or opaque. But remember that it is to be viewed on a flat surface, not standing or hanging.

The working question is "with what?" as you try associating another material with it, beside it, behind it, as background, foil, or companion. Solo qualities become less important than combined qualities, and the combination will take on, for you, a visual unity or "presence," such as tawny-warm-deep, light-scintillating-lively, cool-quiet-delicate. When this feeling appears, you will want to clarify and enrich it by your selection and arrangement of materials. Make additions which bring out, reinforce, or enhance the developing effect. More or fewer of the same materials may be needed; or they may reappear as variations within the whole. Perhaps you will want to add a related material or a dash of the unexpected.

As you move your materials about on the table, experimenting with relationships, you will begin to envision a kind, size, shape, and color of background. It is usually better to confine your materials rather than to have them float about in larger emptiness, but there are no rules about this. The kind of corrugated board from which cartons are made works well and facilitates fastening. You may need to use areas of dark or light or colored paper or cloth on this background; all shapes, colors, and spaces will need consideration as active, contributing parts of your collage.

Your organization may include see-through networks, granular, sprinkled textures, or linear connections. Try working on your visual questions by covering and uncovering parts, asking yourself whether the whole is better with or without, with more or less, here or there, and so on.

Some materials will be changed or eliminated to clarify or strengthen the design. Then you will be ready to fasten things in place so that the collage may be stood vertically for study at a distance. Since you are "working in collage" rather than "making a collage," a minimum of finish and permanence will probably suffice. The making of collages involves many technical problems of fastening; and indeed, the extensive lore of adhesives, pins, and wires can be important information for a teacher of children. Most materials can be pasted to the background, but some will need to be pinned while drops of glue take hold, or fastened with a twist of fine wire poked through the background and taped in back.

If your collage has become somewhat three-dimensional, through such materials as split wood, gathered velvet,

glass beads, or twisted fibers, you may find that a surrounding frame of wood strips will help, not for gran-
deur, but to help in recognizing and establishing the
volume or depth of your collage.

33   *Collage of textured papers.*

Experiment 13:

A Thematic Collage

In Experiment 12, finding materials led to finding the
unifying aesthetic character of the collage composition.
Sometimes, by contrast, the appearance of this unifying character is so strongly suggestive of something
else that a focusing idea or theme takes over. Then the
collage may become an impression (not a picture) of a
hot rod, prim Aunt Kate, or a dark Florida swamp. One
example of such a collage grew out of strong reactions
to an all-day fieldtrip through the back streets, hallways,
and flats of a city's slum district. The collage was not a
scene from that trip but rather a putting together impressions of the day's trash piles, see-through fence slits,
grandiose architectural fragments, cracked and murky

glass, strings of pearly lights, and bright billboards. These were all half-buried suggestions, arranged in a shallow box-frame overcast by a gray/pink haze and laced with a taut web of binding strings.

Try working on a collage which will convey your own feeling about how something is, rather than how it looks in some specific view. You will find that, although some of your materials will help you convey the impression, the way you organize them will help too; for example, they may be crowded or spaced out, formal or informal, busy or quiet.

Working out such a thematic collage depends on a clear over-all feeling, translated into visual form. Without this central feeling as a guide, the arrangement could become only a clever collection of literary allusions; but with a touchstone of feeling, you will find expressing it in collage a direct and satisfying experience.

Taking suggestions from children's ways of working, you may find it easier to move from experimenting with single materials to working out an expressive unity from their interplay if you can respond to the qualities of your found materials *in motion.* Working within a stage frame, with favorable lighting and sound, you may develop a collage which works not only in space but also in time. Two such kinds of collage are described in Chapter 10. They are collage puppets, with animistic overtones, and choreographed collage, which moves to music. Both are based on the fundamental aesthetic experience of finding collage materials.

Questions

1. Cite examples of:
    a. Kinds of questions a child might ask himself as he works effectively in collage.
    b. Verbalized questioning by a teacher which might help (or hinder) his work.
    c. Non-verbalized questioning (implied in teacher's provision and management of materials, time, space, etc.) which might affect child's working.

2. Give examples of ready-made formulas which individuals sometimes apply to their visual design problems. What are possible sources of these mechanical kinds of "logical" routines and procedures?

9

Working with Found Sounds

Although our habits of coarse categorizing tend to wall off the visual arts from other fields such as music, working with found sounds is in many ways similar to working with the found materials of the visual world. Insights gained from ventures into this related art field help teachers to understand children's working processes.

The kind of "name, file, and forget" system which we learn to apply to looking and seeing is even more deadening to our listening and hearing. Young children may retain some pleasure in sounds as sounds while they are necessarily trained in differentiation of sounds as signifiers of other things. Most adults would need to listen deliberately to recapture such response to the "how" as well as the "what" of sounds.

Distinguishing the sound of the neighbor's door from that of one's own is an obviously useful skill, to be judged primarily as the correct or incorrect answer to "What was that?" In arriving at such an answer one may have compared pitches, timbre, resonance, volume, fading, and right/left ear perception. In terms of ordinary functioning these sound elements, while useful as signals, constitute "nonsense" in themselves. However, focusing on the qualities of the sounds around us, without reference to their "significance," may not only refresh our hearing but may also help to throw light on the finding process in many kinds of aesthetic experience and creative work.

34   *Trying out sound-making possibilities of objects.*

Experiment 14:

Finding Sound-Making Objects

A practical way to enter into such work is to hunt for sound-producing objects, preferably portable ones, in the environment. If several people are cooperating in this venture, as is advantageous, each should find several such objects whose qualities he finds interesting. To discover such a quality may require considerable experimenting. For example, a small cream pitcher may emit one percussive pitch when a forefinger is clapped across its top opening, and another if two fingers are used; or an enamelware wash basin may need to be suspended by a string rather than held or rested on a table, and it may sound better struck with a knuckle than with a stick. In this experimenting the purpose would be to discover the special sound-making possibilities of the object and how they may best be realized. The finder brings a found object to the group less as delivery than as sponsorship: "Let me introduce my friend who . . ."

The exploration is helped if a range of different kinds of sound can be included. The ringing pitches of struck objects may be extended to include the soft thud of a broom on a chair seat; in other words hunt for fading and non-fading percussive sounds. There are continuing, regular sounds, as from chains, bubbling water, stroked corrugated surfaces, grids, or rough fabrics, and there is continuous irregularity in the sound of crumpling paper or a rock rolling down a steep, rough hill.

In this kind of hunt it is best to avoid all musical instruments, such as pianos, recorders, or drums because, by their strong associations, they tend to dominate and to narrow the field of listening. Even found sounds with too distinct pitch, such as bells, may prove distracting. Vocal sounds, too, should be saved for experimentation other than a sound-making hunt.

Acoustical analysis of sound differences, itself quite controversial, may be cited to separate noises from music; but again our selection should be based on the direct response of liking or interest in sound quality, not on its causes. Ignoring science is certainly no requirement for aesthetic experience, but the satisfaction of erecting informational structures, especially authoritative, limited ones, may reduce the appetite for direct sensing. Thus a teacher may bypass listening in order to inform his students about sound waves or hearing.

If finding sounds were made the goal of listening and hearing, it would tend to limit the process by stressing the satisfaction or feeling of fulfillment in a complete experience. To some extent this is part of most collecting. Only in playing a sound along with and over against others, from the same or different sources, in composed combinations and sequences, does one really find its qualities. In other words, *in order to find, one must relate.*

Experiment 15:

Relating Sounds in Improvised Compositions

Two things, partners and a tape recorder, facilitate this experiment. The advantage of having one or more partners is partly that one person cannot work with several sound-making instruments at once, and partly the multiplication of discovered sound materials and ideas. If the work of composition were carried to the level of fine decisions (and work with found sounds can reach this level) then the composing would have to be done by an individual. But in early stages it is more likely that members of a small group can stimulate and support each other and also work out a satisfying improvised arrangement with the sounds they have found. Large numbers of people, as in some classes, would need to be divided into groups of four or so and given enough physical distance or separation so that each group could hear only its own sounds.

The screening which each one has already given to the sounds he has found will help, so that he will not be bringing interesting objects but rather he will be reporting interesting sound possibilities for the work of the group. Similarities will appear, some as suggestive variations in families of sound, some as mere repetitions. Certain sounds will have a unique, solo character, while others will suggest a connecting overlay or background. Some sounds will combine well, converse back and forth, or suggest a building up in layers or sequences. The one requirement in working is to *listen,* making use of the original sound qualities. Increasing involvement in working with the sounds will gradually displace preoccupation with irrelevant associations of the objects. For example, the fact that all of the objects may have come from a kitchen or from a chemistry laboratory would not affect the sound composition. Listening may be helped by not watching the sound production and by reducing the light in the room.

Recording

Before long a general plan for an improvised composition, perhaps a minute or two in length, will be developed and ready for recording on tape. Slight sounds, as of tissue paper, may need to be produced near the microphone, with others, like those from sheet metal, placed at a distance. Hearing a tape recording has the great advantage of eliminating visual distractions; it will make clear to the group what they have found and may show how the design can be improved.

Experiment 16:

Diagrammatic Notation

As members of a small sound-making group move from hearing individual sounds to hearing relationships, passages, and patterns of sound, they will be able to improvise more effectively. Some may follow such work by designing compositions individually for performance by a group. To do this some kind of diagramming of sequences, combinations, and development will help the composer to explain his intentions to his performing partners. A great variety of graphic means can be invented for this purpose. Adopting such standard conventions as a left-to-right time dimension, and bottom-to-top as low-to-high pitch is one way to begin, but composers experimenting with colored chalks, papers, and other media on large sheets or strips of paper will find many ways to indicate their intentions to their fellow performers without attempting complete notation.

35   *Five part "Dirge for Prepositions."*

Using a tape recorder to play back found-sound compositions will suggest to some experimenters possibilities of finding new sounds among the found sounds by manipulating tapes. With two tape recorders and varied speeds, one can greatly enlarge the expressive scope of his sound materials, as has been shown by many composers. Reference to record libraries or to catalogs of recorded music will help the student of sound to find many works in related fields, developed by recognized composers during the last fifty years.*

Hearing some of these compositions may serve to direct the interest of the listening beginner toward an understanding participation in the expressive statements of great composers in all media and will show him that novelty of source is unimportant compared to meaningful form. He will find this form achieved intuitively by such design processes as stating, varying, echoing, conversing, subordinating, overlapping, increasing, diminishing, recalling, following, uniting, opposing, and many others all reflecting aspects of everyday human experience.

Probably more valuable to the individual as an outgrowth of working with found sounds would be an increased responsiveness to qualitative differences in sounds and in sound patterns and relationships as they occur in the environment. Making some

---

*Recordings which feature *Musique Concrete* compositions (manipulation of recorded sounds, as opposed to sounds created by electronic means) would probably come closest to the experiments with found sounds; a great range is available. See *Sounds of New Music,* Folkways Records. FX6160.

kind of notes, verbal or graphic, to record one's responses to these heard discoveries may lead to useful exchanges among listeners and may further reveal a constructive aspect of sensory experience previously limited to cognition.

Spoken Sound

From working with found sounds produced by objects one may become interested in experimenting with other kinds of sounds. One of these is exploring the possibilities of *spoken sound* and developing, recording, and playing back compositions for small groups of speaking voices. While this work comes most naturally as an aspect of the reading, writing, and speaking of poetry, it is also closely related to music.*

36   *Sampling Toch's "Geography" for four speaking voices.*

Increased understanding of the compositions of Varese, Cage, or Schoenberg, or the poetry of Hopkins, Cummings, or Williams, is probably less important as an outcome of our work with found sounds or sounds of speech than is our sharpened awareness of the qualities of sounds as we hear them in interplay on the street or playground, or in the home or classroom. In addition to seeing that many things can be materials for inventive reorganization, we learn as teachers that many situations are open to revised, more imaginative exploration and enjoyment. Both kinds of work start with consideration of certain "givens" and add the variables of individual experience, thought, feeling, and purpose.

Isolating certain aspects of the environment, such as surface relief or spoken sound, helps us approach them freshly as working materials. But one of the most exciting uses of found materials comes from combining visual stuffs with recorded passages of instrumental music in a moving collage type of puppetless puppet show. This is described in Chapter 10.

---

*A famous example of *spoken music* is Ernst Toch's *Geographical Fugue,* written in 1930 and available in a Decca recording by the Abbey Singers, DL10073.

10

Materials Come Alive as Puppets

"It's not the thing, it's the wiggle." That is the first law of puppetry, as anyone knows who has brought to life a limp pile of cloth, wood, and other fibers. In the finding of aesthetic materials, the "wiggle" is the expressive quality which the finder sees in the "thing." And creating a composition with those found qualities means bringing them to life. In collage this is the process of finding the unifying character and evocative impact rising out of the interaction of those qualities.

Unlike the carefully objective observation and analysis of science, the finding in aesthetic/creative work infuses the thinking/feeling experience of the individual into the materials. Textiles, for example, are a main interest of many people throughout the world, and no doubt this interest always includes some degree of both technological analysis and aesthetic response. The special aesthetic character of fabrics is known not only from seeing and touching them but from handling and moving them to see how they hang, fall, soften, hug, reveal, hide, sweep, crumple, tumble, fold, whip, wrinkle, billow, and swirl. Thus in action one discovers their capacity for expressive behavior. Sometimes textiles partake of landscape or setting, as in the caverns, hills, and ridges of one's bedding. Sometimes they convert one into another person, as with the turban, cowl, cape, or train. And who does not recall the warm, comfortable fit of "dirty" clothes and the assertive crispness of their clean successors?

The kinds of expressive character found in fabrics appear in many other stuffs as interaction and involvement with them develop. Boards, weeds, papers, and ropes all offer special qualities in action. To discover these, it is essential that the finder give himself generously to responsive play with these materials.

The exhilaration and the uncertainty of aesthetic experience are in many ways like exploring a foreign land; in both instances one may see more in the company of friends.

How these interpersonal advantages contribute to working with found materials may be shown in two kinds of experimental puppetry. Starting in individual play with materials, they lead into identification with their expressive qualities and then into projection of the found character in improvised interaction with other "characters."

The first of these experiments is a playful departure from the work with collage described in Chapter 8. While it can result in some degree of theatrical "production," our purpose in trying it is to highlight the aesthetic experience of finding and composing with materials.

Experiment 17:

Collage Puppets

Although this experiment can involve any number of people, it works best in small groups or sub-groups, as in a class or a family: some young participants are an asset.

Puppetry improvisation invites a kind of gradual, open transition from individual finding and inventing to interpersonal exchange. How much and when it becomes group work can vary if pre-determined performance goals are avoided.

Everyone should contribute to the supply of *collage materials,* including bits of solid colored, patterned, and textured cloths, papers, and other surfaces. Although quantities can be small, a wide range is helpful.

The second requirement is a supply of *cardboard,* as heavy as can be cut with scissors. Chipboard, newsboard, or laundry shirt boards will do well. Scraps and pieces cut by a paper cutter or left from other projects are useful. The following additional materials, tools and equipment will be needed:

scissors
stapler
paper punch or awl (a nail will do)
paper fasteners, #3
paste or white glue
tongue depressors or other sticks, with ⅛ inch hole drilled at one end.

As we shall see later, nothing on this list is indispensable. However, considering some of the ingredients as "givens" helps to focus the attention on the "variables," in this case the collage materials. Presenting steps in the working procedure can give a similar priority to the central work with the expressive possibilities of these materials.

In preliminary collecting of collage materials, one can sometimes find suggestions of character direction, such as slinky, regal, or raucous; more often these appear later. Usually the experimenter begins with pieces of cardboard, choosing and assembling scraps to form some kind of "creature," all except its legs, fins, or wings. One should avoid elaborate cutting and shaping of the cardboard, since a precise silhouette is unimportant. Stapling two or three well-chosen scraps together will usually suffice. The height of this "body" should be kept under eight or ten inches, since lofty figures tend to become top-heavy.

Next, two holes are punched near the bottom of the cardboard figure, not too close together, and the tongue depressor blade legs are fastened on with paper fasteners. Then its running is tested by moving the legs (see Figure 38).

With the foundation thus prepared and movement provided for, the main work with the collage materials begins. First, different kinds of cloth or other stuffs are considered for covering the creature's larger surfaces; then, appropriate additional materials are tried out and applied.

37 *Cardboard scraps are stapled together and fitted with legs.*

38 *Locomotion is tried out on stage.*

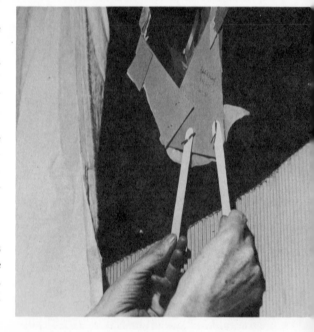

39   *A talkative, twitchy hen.*

40   *Sophisticated adventurer.*

From the beginning the question arises, "Who is this?" along with "What is he like, how does he move, think, talk, behave?" Such speculation is kept tentative, but the point is that a whole "being" is beginning to appear, mainly as a result of the choice and arrangement of collage materials.

As decisions are made, the materials, including trimmings and highlights, are pasted, glued, or stapled on to the cardboard. Usually only one side is covered, but if both sides are done the puppet can later appear "going either north or south." Some things, like buttons or pine cones, are fastened on more easily with fine wire than with glue or laborious sewing. The tongue depressor legs may need to be covered or even replaced. Feet are usually omitted since the creature will appear above and from behind a wall or screen and will be moved by the leg control sticks.

Bringing Puppets to Life

The characters will soon be sufficiently developed to begin getting acquainted. Fish, princesses, dogs, boys, birds, and unknown species will appear, but *who* or what they are is less important than *how* they are (noisy, timid, cuddly, oratorical, and so on). And this quality, determined earlier by choice of materials, now affects their ways of acting.

This phase of "bringing to life" is an essential part of the working experience by the person who constructs the puppet. Possible movements need to be explored; learning to take steps is especially important, and better than pumping or jerking the puppet up and down. Subtle movements, like heaving a sigh, should be tried, in addition to bounding and running.

The sooner the operating can take place from behind some kind of screen, the better. Practicing in front of a mirror helps to remind the operator of the visual character of his puppet.

Although stage provisions may vary, the essential is a screen for the operator to work behind and for the puppet to appear above. Designs for practical puppet stages are described in the Appendix, p. 185.

A helper "out front" can warn when operators' hands show, the puppet is too low, or its voice is inaudible.

Learning to operate this kind of stick puppet will proceed quickly. Their limited expressive movements make long speeches unsuitable. The speaking puppet can be indicated by moving him with his syllables and phrases and, especially, by the others' stillness when they are listening. But the puppets' howls, shivers, whimpers and roars may say more than their words. For this reason ready-made stories or gags are less useful than improvising within some simple situation suggested by the characters themselves; and dramatic skits should be held to one or two minutes in length.

Since talking usually takes priority in the adult's attention, the operator may find himself "thinking of things to say" and saying them while his puppet jerks aimlessly. In this case, one must remember that the puppet, not the operator, must do the talking. What the puppet has to express is inherent in its nature; imposed cleverness will not help. As the operator gradually attunes himself to the puppet's behavior, he will find himself looking at his puppet rather than at the other operators. Repeating a conversation silently, with the word sounds only imagined, will improve timing and movement, and will clarify the visual expressiveness of the puppets. Even though there is no formal production for an audience other than fellow experimenters, it is advisable to work with a puppet until it seems to behave somewhat autonomously. The wholeness of a complex character, sought earlier in the more static visual terms of collage, is still the aim of our finding and using aesthetic materials in this creative invention.

To use these visual materials only for a literary departure would short circuit the kind of work with materials which the experiment is designed to encourage. It would certainly limit the experience for anyone who might find himself carrying out an assigned speaking role. At

41   *Operator backstage.*

42   *On-stage conversation.*

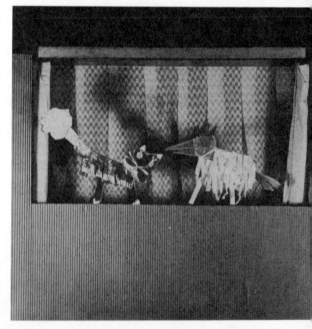

the same time it should be stressed that for non-English speaking children collage puppertry, with its sensory appeals to the imagination and its shielded projection, has provided to be a remarkably effective invitation not only to express themselves in the new language, but to speak with a great range of personal feeling.

The instructions for experimenting with collage puppets have been specified rather completely in order to focus most of the aesthetic experience and creative work on "bringing found materials to life." This central part of the work has been left open to allow free discovery and invention. In practice such an experiment could be carried out in one or, at most, two working periods.

There will be many departures from these instructions. For example, some materials may prove more expressive as three-dimensional characters than as flat collage. Thus an unadorned length of black boa, moved by a couple of wire loops, can become feline grace itself.

43   *Paper bags become all-around hand puppets.*

Other Puppets

There are many other kinds of "quick puppets" which teachers find useful with children, such as paper bag, sock, vegetable, and newspaper-paste hand puppets, as well as shadow, rod, and string puppets. They are described in books listed in the Bibliography, pp.201. Less well known among these are rod puppets. Life size or larger, they are used in outdoor shows and parades. Their heads are paper sculpture or cartons, mounted on light rods. From these rods hang their costumes, usually cast-off, full-size clothing. Other rods, such as bamboo poles, and perhaps a few strings may be used to operate the puppets' hands, jaws, or eyes.

Another kind of puppetry has grown out of playful "casting" of friends and acquaintances, asking, "What kind of vegetable (or fruit) is he (or she)?" This has led to marionettes made of vegetables and fruit and controlled by strings, such as an eggplant school board member, pineapple principal, rutabaga coach, celery English teacher, and so on.

Experiment 18:

Choreographed Collage or "Junk Ballet"

A second kind of puppetry, not widely known, is included here because it provides, especially for adults, an

unusually stimulating approach to using aesthetic qualities in found materials. Unlike collage puppets, it does
not associate materials with such realistic or fantastic
"characters," nor do the "puppets" express themselves in
words. Instead, the materials become abstract dancing
elements whose character and movement are suggested
by music.

Groups which have enjoyed experimenting wth this
kind of moving collage have included family-plus-
neighbors, rural as well as urban school teachers, and
children and adults with varied experience in the arts.
Since most of them had been doing some previous experimental work with collage, they had at least a beginning collection of found materials and some experience in their use.

The group begins its work by listening to music, usually
records; access to a good record collection or library is
helpful. Depending on the time available, the group can
hunt for suitable music or choose from a pre-selected list
of records.

Certain kinds of music have proved to be more useful
than others. Instrumental music is usually better than
vocal, especially if the latter has story-telling lyrics. Similarly, certain titles, as in some program music, are better
avoided or concealed if they suggest specific images, objects, or characters such as birds, horsemen, pine trees, or
mountains. The most desirable music has strongly de-
lineated sounds, either from contrasting instrumental
voices or from the structure of the composition itself.
What is sought, at least in the beginning, is a brief excerpt from a longer composition which has clearly differentiated characteristics, both in its sound elements
and in the whole passage.

In listening, such questions as the following may be applied to the music: does it seem light, dark, slow, fast,
bright, severe, sinuous, clumsy, delicate, ragged, thin,
rich, stark, luminous? In short, the members of the
group ask themselves the key question, "How is it?",
seeking descriptions which may be expressed visually.

The group will not need to agree on all details. Wide disagreement might indicate that the music is too ambivalent for this experiment and that something simpler is needed. On the other hand, the music should sustain interest throughout the experiment.

As with any group invention, authoritative opinions by any one member, including the teacher, should be avoided. Although such dictates may help production, they may also endanger learning by reducing individual responsibility. Everyone accustomed to the kind of decision making and problem solving in which answers fit exactly may have difficulty in seeking what "feels right," on a scale ranging from "Nothing happens" to "Wonderful!" Keeping choices tentative will help individuals to play the interested hunches required for genuine creative work.

In this experiment the group is working toward a visual interpretation, parallel or equivalent to the music, to be stated as a moving collage wihin a shallow, three-dimensional stage behind a proscenium frame.* The variables which give it life are found materials, light, space, sound, and time.

When music is tentatively selected, the listening question "How is it?" moves on to "Like what . . . ?" and to trying some material, such as the rising folds of a chenille bedspread, or a hanging, slowly turning white ball, or the rough weight of an overturned butter tub, painted dark red. Moving or operating the materials may need to be accomplished from above, below, or from either end of the "stage."

Having one or two strong lights, such as a spotlight or a slide projector, will be a great help, as is the ability to modify the intensity and color of the light with dimmers and gelatines. Work could begin, however, with simple lighting such as a desk lamp.

Depending on the size of the proscenium, somewhat larger pieces of material will be needed than for most

---

*Suggestions for constructing a suitable stage frame are in the Appendix, p. 185.

of the work on collages or collage puppets described earlier in this chapter.

A stage curtain which can be closed will help to keep the visualized musical excerpt within the context of a whole composition or movement. This becomes important if the group goes on to present its work for an audience, as for other groups within a class. If the music is unfamiliar to the audience, the whole recorded composition should be played with curtains closed and then replayed with curtains opening during the chosen part and closing during the rest of the music. This arrangement reduces the ill effects of excerpting.

Sometimes there are advantages in using the beginning section of a musical composition, during its first statement of musical ideas, rather than the more complex later development. The strong rhythmic beat of some music may demand response, but in other cases the rhythmic time pattern will be less insistent. Kinds of music which have been found stimulating and workable include small combinations of jazz instruments, some orchestral ballet music, program music, and twentieth-century experimental music, especially short compositions. Among the composers whose recorded works have proved useful in past ventures with moving collage are Bartok, Hindemith, Holst, Milhaud, Villa Lobos, Carter, and Stravinsky.

After working with moving collage, one's listening to music comes to include noting analogous relationships of moving color, texture, light, shape, space, and so on.

It will occur to members of the group that, rather than relate their moving collage to ready-made music, the music might be composed along with the collage or even following the collage. Thus one group found themselves simply humming an improvised accompaniment as they projected colored shadows of their moving hands on the stage backdrop.

The extent to which decisions can be kept open depends, of course, on the size and experience of the group and on the time available. A small group of interested individuals sharing residence or easy access to a working setup could experiment informally, widely, and deeply. However, a large group, working in only one session, may more easily reach the central questions of the work by being subdivided into smaller groups and being assigned one pre-selected musical composition. Each small group would need a mockup proscenium to work behind and a chance to work in a more fully equipped stage. Such a procedure has resulted in a remarkable variety of visual interpretations of one piece of music.

It is interesting to compare the kind of participation and involvement which individuals put into the choreographed collage or "junk ballet" with that which they give to the collage puppets described earlier. The difference probably lies in how much and how early one needs to bring his ideas into productive harmony with those of his fellow experimenters. With collage puppets each individual eventually finds himself holding on to the two handles of what he has developed as his own invention, more or less ready to help it move and speak with creatures invented by others. Interaction, which does not begin until each unique puppet has been made, can be freely improvised, without any imposed structure of timing.

Junk ballet, on the other hand, begins with agreement on the musical selection. Thereafter, members of the group may participate in many different ways, but they will have the same musical passage as a common reference point. What simplifies the working process and makes it worthwhile is the shared appetite for discovery. The thrill of working in choreographed collage comes from a feeling of rightness in a visualized realization of exciting music. Some examples of how groups have worked may help to explain the process:

—When an operator cascaded a mailing tubeful of colored glass marbles into the bright light of the stage, he felt he had found just the equivalent for the scintillating arpeggios of a jazz piano.

—The second movement of *Music for Strings, Percussion, Celeste,* by Bela Bartok,* was chosen because it seemed dark and mysterious. The opening repetition of one staccato note on the xylophone suggested a flashing light, set high in the dark backdrop. Then, as a viola introduced the major theme, an operator sitting below the stage thrust up a curving, metallic blade as its visual parallel, following it with a second, larger blade (to the sound of a second, more insistent viola) rising and turning in horizontal bands of light.

—Another group also chose a "dark" beginning: the section of Holst's *Planets* called *Saturn.*** The experimenters found that dark cloth stretched across the lower part of the stage opening could be turned into moving, breathing mountains by stroking from below with upthrust coat hangers.

—A wild, coarse, background chant of men's voices led to a crude lattice woven out of swamp grasses. Its pulsating shadow was projected onto the backdrop. The soaring soprano (of Yma Sumac) was a suspended white disk, turning and rising into the changing light.

—Boards, boxes, and light bulbs, operated by sticks and strings from above, below, and the ends of the stage, were chosen to present a short, pounding section of Mossolov's *Steel Foundry.****

In each case response to the music led to ideas, experiments with materials, and choices of what seemed to "work" best. The examples above are cited only to encourage the reader to find his own unique solutions.

In earlier chapters certain questions have been raised concerning the effect which end-product emphasis can have on aesthetic experience. It is apparent that both collage puppets and, especially, choreographed collage may become subject to that kind of conclusive emphasis, as public performance becomes their goal. If such sharing is limited to fellow experimenters, the learning experience can be kept more open.

Similar questions have been raised concerning the possible effects of working in group situations, and here the two puppetry experiments were found to be somewhat

*Columbia recording ML-5979, among others.
**RCA recording: Holst, G., *The Planets,* BBC Symphony Orchestra, LHMV 1002.
***Folkways Record, FX 6160.

different. Both have been presented primarily as extensions of the process of "finding materials," for example, in studying how different kinds of cloth behave. As aesthetic experience, this finding has demanded personal involvement in the qualities of environmental stuffs. How such finding may lead one on into the processes of creative work has also been suggested: the experimenter could bring to life the qualities found in materials only if he could "go with" the character or the developing qualities which he found. This kind of generous identification is the heart of any aesthetic/creative work and is the basis of the different kind of experiment discussed in the next chapter.

SECTION II

11

Enriching Aesthetic Response

There is growing public concern about cultural deprivation in early childhood and its effect on later learning. The programs being developed to correct such poverty may also contribute to public understanding of the whole job of growing up and how it can be helped. The child's health is now seen as an individual combination or pattern of many closely related factors. Less well understood is the kind of learning experience which will improve the child's ability to meet new ones.

Our concern with "enabling" kinds of experiences for young children is accompanied by widespread interest in new techniques for more efficient training in specific, pre-determined skills. Children are now able to learn more such skills and to learn them faster by mechanical processes which tell them, in effect, "Perform this *and only this* operation with this *and only this* material." Beginning with a precise statement of the foreseen end product (what is to be learned), designer/engineers apply rigorous analysis to circuit-like processes of the nervous system as it works with series of isolated, uncluttered questions or program steps. Such techniques are bringing increased effectiveness to long-recognized processes of training and conditioning in performance of specific skills. Making such new skill-training equipment as talking typewriters accessible to young children could support a great educational advance, *provided we take advantage of this help to turn toward the larger task before us.* That is the task of helping children incorporate their skills into the complex, individual, open-ended processes of education. The ability to read will help to give them access to a heritage, but they must still learn to re-create that heritage.

As in so many other fields, the technological improvements which we bring to one part of education are producing new challenges for other parts. Despite the inefficiency in school work which allowed speeding-up, delaying, skipping, waiting, concentrating, detouring, persevering, or quitting, the comparative openness of pacing in these former methods, even in class drill, also allowed some freedom to "work around" with the materials and to incorporate them into individual experience.

44   *Learning to stay with his own questioning.*

45   *Clay is inviting stuff.*

Now, as certain parts of the curriculum become more effectively programmed for impersonal training in correct performance, other parts which emphasize personal perception and creative construction must be greatly strengthened and enriched.

Classroom teachers are in a position to know that aesthetic experience is a qualitative ingredient possible in any part of the school day, and that whenever children stop to ask themselves, "What is this, *really?*" they may also reach out for, take, remake, and incorporate into their own individual thinking/feeling experience the essential materials of education.* Here the product, much to be desired, is the child's

---

*See Appendix, p. 197, "Criteria for Planning Children's Creative Art Projects Which Are Related to Other Curriculum Areas."

increased ability to stay with his own questioning—in other words, to involve himself generously in self-assigned play. Although discovery is still the main purpose, it may take place most importantly in continued play with the simplest materials.

Some parents and teachers outdo even the manufacturers and dealers in their faith in the hardware and equipment of education—faith that disadvantage can be cured by *things* and that head starts can be founded on things. Since this faith in things is sometimes accompanied by a genuine valuing of children's individuality, we should not exaggerate the damage or waste from ordering one of everything on an approved list. But we should help the friends of children to focus on and to question the quality of learning experience which results from working with the "things" of education.

For both children and adults, the desirability of having little or much to work with probably depends on the quality of the having. We saw earlier in such experiments with found materials as *collage* that the range of stuffs one can usefully draw upon depends largely on the finding and sharing process which has helped to make them one's own materials. Thoughtful choosing does not depend on the number of alternatives. It was also pointed out that a material (what one works with) need not be any kind of tangible, physical stuff.

Many important aesthetic experiences come from continued, deepening involvement with very simple materials. Compositions may be created not only out of different stuffs but also out of the different possibilities of one stuff. Continuing work is then based on increasingly rewarding interaction with the material; and the richness of the working process comes more and more from the worker. To call forth such sustained, growing response, a material must first offer clarity of character as a vehicle for one's statements without suggesting that it could itself be a complete statement.

One of the most clearly inviting stuffs is clay, the kind of moist modeling clay used in ceramics.* Experiments described earlier, in Chapter 5, used clay as the accepting stuff into which many found embossing materials were pressed in creating relief surfaces or "fossils," but in the experimental work which follows, clay becomes the means through which we can identify ourselves with the muscular world of three-dimensional sculpture. From reaching out into the environment to discover many materials we turn now to inner resources for enriched aesthetic experience with one material.

---

*The full scope of what clay offers as a material cannot be experienced without firing. This is one of many rewarding processes which the plan and purpose of this book must exclude, but the opportunity to sense firsthand the excitement of this elemental transformation should be made available to everyone old enough to peer at his clay work in the fury of the kiln. The difference between the beginner's ash tray as experience and the expressive mastery of the great potter is a difference in depth and richness of individual working experience, and clay and fire are only instruments, although powerful ones, in achieving that difference.

12

Experiment in Response to Three-Dimensional Form Through Clay

Because it is handled directly, clay offers unique advantages. No intermediate steps or tools separate us from it.

Experiment 19:

Responding to Mass and Posture

Start with about two pounds of clay of the right consistency—not so dry that a coil around your finger cracks, nor so wet that it sticks to your hands. Work

at a table which can be cleaned easily, and get a work board or tile to allow for easy, continued turning of your work. Water and tools other than your hands will not be needed until much later.

First, pick up your chunk of clay and work with it simply to find out what the stuff is like and how it behaves. Beyond the tactile sensations of cool, damp softness, see how it responds to squeezing, poking, patting, pounding. Restore it to a lumpish ball and drop it on the work board. Observe how it plops down with a kind of thud and seems to offer no resistance. It acts the way we do when, thoroughly exhausted and completely relaxed, we fall in a heap, with not one muscle working. Clay's undifferentiated mass, unity around a central point, simply surrenders to gravity. Now turn the board and you will begin to see its three-dimensional solid form.

46   *Direct response to touch and pressure.*

48   *Rising—reaching.*

47   *The point of a blob is its center.*

Next, draw up or elongate the clay, so that it starts to project up from the board; no longer an inert blob, it rises. Continue until out of the centrally organized mass of its former ball shape it reaches up vertically as high as it will stand with stability. Its inside sense, or "internal dynamics," has shifted from a mid-point centrality to the linear axis of the vertical, like the body experience of standing, reaching, straining upward.

Try tipping the straight axis form, more and more, until, to prevent its falling on its face, a counter balance, or supporting prop, restores its stability. Its internal linearity, or strong sense of direction, is still its main feature, *no matter how the outside surface looks.*

Now, to modify the force of the axis, try curving it. Or change the axis from a single swoop to a broken, jagged, linear movement, like the dodging drive of a football player, or to a combination of broken line and curve.

In all these changes, you should turn the clay work almost constantly to avoid visual fixation on any particular side. Always resist the temptation to slick up the form's surfaces, which would distract your attention from study of its internal forces.

The clay's characteristically clumsy weight will remain part of the form, and the reaching, pushing, or curving of that form will be occurring within *clay,* not within boards, wires, or metal sheets.

More questions about the clay should be raised. From its first blob-like form, we know it tends to sit on a broad bottom, like a pyramid. But need this be? Try raising the clay, heavy and soft though it is, so it rises and reaches out from a smaller perch or footing.

Try fastening two masses of clay together, keeping the character of each somewhat independent while welding them into a unity, again studied from all sides.

Without slicking with water, try variations in planes (flat, full, concave) and in their edges and junctures.

Sometimes we limit the form possibilities of clay by limiting our handling of it. For example, if our fingers only poke or pinch it or if they stroke over and over along its valleys, we may be honoring mostly our fingers, with the clay form only their hollowed, sharp-ridged imprint. If instead we seek a convex roundness, then patting or rubbing *around* its hills may emphasize their massive emergence from cores and axes within the clay.

49   *Experiencing linear axes in movement.*

50   *Directional force is understood in action.*

What we are investigating is the basic aesthetic nature
of a material. In raising questions with the clay we have
tried to find out what it likes to do, what kinds of expressive action are most natural to it, how it behaves.
As we have worked we have also seen forms developing
in a way *we* like, suggesting possibilities for further
study and control. If and when these leads appear, we
follow them to see what forms we can work out with
the clay.

This working process is different from deciding what to make and then judging
our work right or wrong as it resembles or differs from that authoritative "thing out
there" which we are trying to reproduce. Such an idea may handicap aesthetic/creative
work because the noun name of the planned thing tends to be everybody's noun
name, committing the worker to produce a kind of archetype or stereotype, as generally acceptable as correct spelling. In contrast, seeing the thing begin to appear in
one's clay has the advantage, first, of being individually "found" and, moreover, of
appearing almost inevitably in a special, expressive version. Thus, if one were to see
a whale in the clay, there would be a good chance that one wanted to see it and also
that it would appear not just as a "type" whale, but as a specific one, such as a grace-
ful whale, a fighting whale, a diving whale, a lazy whale—and given enough experience, as one's own *clay* whale. Because our interest is in aesthetic/creative experience,
we would probably be less concerned with details of whale anatomy or even with
over-all "whaleness" than with such expressive qualities as gracefulness or pugnacity.
We might even seek to form in clay such a quality alone.

For the purpose of our experiment, the choice of a representational or abstract
goal is less important than the hundreds of working choices, large and small, made
in the process. Handling should be slow and patient and should be subordinated to
looking, lest busy fingers smooth over unobserved possibilities of form. Looking is
helped by turning, and when new leads are needed, by looking from a new vantage
point: from farther away, from above, below, or with different lighting. But the
crucial view is from *inside* the clay, which means responding kinesthetically to the
way the clay form works—rising, leaning, turning, looming, jutting, hanging, ex-
panding, guarding, brooding, binding, bracing—in short, in seeing its form with
understanding, the artist *becomes* it in terms of muscular body state. If it feels
"neither this way nor that," it probably needs to be simplified, pulled toether, made
whole by a main unifying movement. One's eyes and hands are the best tools for
seeing and making, but the muscles of shoulders, legs, arms, and neck help one's
knowing the three-dimensional forces at work in the form.

Clay is so suggestible, so easily changed, that you may wish you could stop,
freeze, or hold your work at some stage. Photography, especially movies, may help a
little, and so will scribbled sketches aimed at recording masses, not boundary-like outlines. Casting is a laborious process, but it can record the work product. Firing should

not be an afterthought but an elemental part of the clay's first forming.* Simply letting the clay work dry slowly will allow it to remain for future study, even though it may be very fragile. Of course, the main products or results will be stored visual memories and increased responsiveness to sculptural form.

Responding to Massive Form in the Environment

Sometimes we see a child drawing himself up straight as he looks at some tall vertical, or tipping his head or torso in accord with the slant of whatever he is observing. This kinesthetic identification may play a less active part in our adult response to the things around us. This usually occurs because the quickest possible recognition is all the response we can afford as we scurry on our way.

If we stop to look at other people, such as someone sleeping on a park bench or someone pushing a car, our empathy with the curving back or straining shoulders may be a part of a narrative or associative process—when did he go to sleep, will his muscles ache tomorrow, we should check our gas, and so on. Some story telling extension may take precedence over our direct response to the shape or posture of other living things like a sunflower, a sway-backed horse, or a plane's fuselage. But muscular identification is probably experienced most clearly in response to such natural shapes as mountains, clouds, bones, tree trunks, or such man-made objects as chairs, tools, jugs, sport cars, or tableware. Life history and useful function are to be seen in such things, of course, but what we seek now is to *participate in them as form*. To do this we go on a hunt for solid, three-dimensional forms.

Within our homes, out the window, on the street, in the country, we look for massive, three-dimensional things interesting for their shape, separating that shapeness from all such irrelevancies as color, texture, size, material, rareness, monetary value, and so on. Often this will mean overlooking parts or details and responding instead to the over-all mass, as of a clump of trees or a sprawling barn. Responding will involve some sensing of how it goes or what it does, both in the axial, directional sense of standing, leaning, or lying, and in the mass surrounding this inner axis. Scribbling crude sketches may help clarify this kind of response, even though the reduction of three-dimensionality to the flat surface of paper is an extreme abstraction. Let your scribbling hand indicate, with many strokes, the inside core or axis or center, and then scribble its mass around it. The purpose of such drawing is to note how a thing works, not how it looks.

Experiment 20:

Form From Inside Forces

This experiment provides an exciting way to study form as internal forces inscribe, project, and expand it in

---

*Methods and provisions for children's clay work in the classrooms are discussed in the Appendix, p. 191.

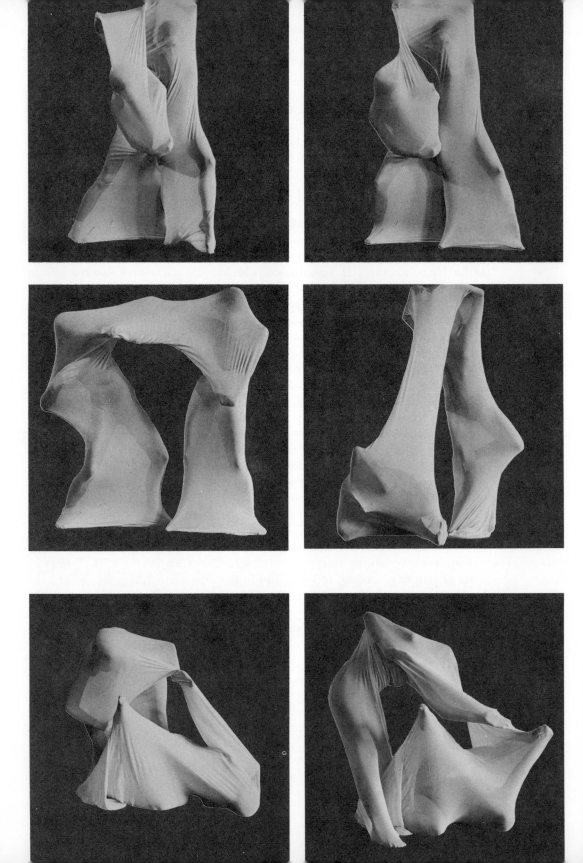

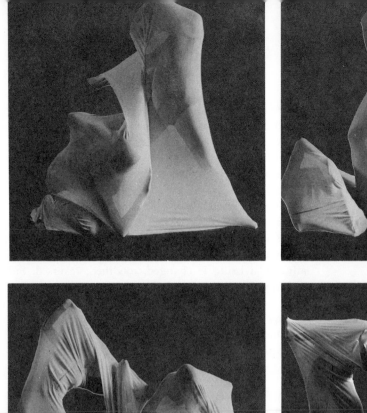

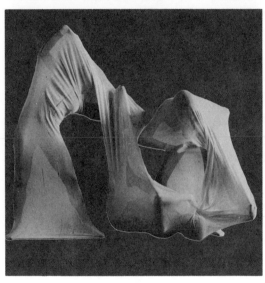

51   *Sculptural form inscribed and projected by internal forces.*

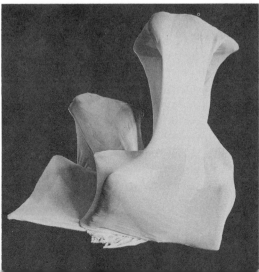

three dimensions. It requires a length of tubular jersey, preferably eight or nine yards long. Lightweight synthetic material stretches better than cotton or wool. The illustrations show how two or three persons, with some of the body awareness and control of the trained dancer, entered the tubing from opposite ends and touched hands at the center. Then, directed partly by those outside and moving slowly and steadily, one may rise and reach out in a strong direction while the partner curves down, around, and outward as a counter force. Gradually the massing is changed, modified, reversed. Side lighting may help reveal the sculptural shape of fullness, hollows, column-like connections, and enclosed shadows, but its purpose is less to illuminate externalized beauty of form than to sense it as an expression of form produced from within.

The kind of body response we have been examining is fundamental not only to our perception of three-dimensional form but also to our feeling about it. Thus, jutting crags and rolling hills call up a wealth of different kinesthetic and emotional associations.

Of course, other factors contribute to the experiencing of three-dimensionality, such as the depth perception based on the converging lines of vision of our eyes, multiplied to an infinity of assimilated views as we move around and about the observed object. And in Chapter 6 we examined the perception of depth as a progression into an object from an assumed front plane. Later on, in Chapters 17 and 18, we shall view the three-dimensional world from within, as an environmental setting in space.

Participating in Sculpture

The field of sculpture is so tremendously varied, both in its formal means and in its feeling content, that one must ask of each kind of sculpture, and finally of each individual piece of sculpture, how it works and how one is to work with it. Practically, this means giving some time to looking at it and "getting with it" until the terms of its ordering, its internal lawfulness, are understood. Unlike the more or less cluttered, accidental shapes found occurring in the environment, great sculpture is the highly selected, organized statement of an experienced, self-disciplined artist.

Probably no one could bring an equally generous response to each of the different kinds of sculpture to be seen in galleries and museums. But tastes do not remain static if they are used, and what meant little earlier may come to mean much through new experience.

The kind of muscularity within solid form which we have been studying characterizes a great range of sculpture. It is worth a great effort to come into the physical presence of the sculpture itself, rather than to rely on inadequately experiencing sculpture through photographs.

Try to take part in Egyptian figures, tiny pre-Columbian figures, sculpture from early Greece and Crete, from Africa and so on. Work with the landmark sculpture of our own century—Rodin, Maillol, Brancusi, Arp, Moore, Lipschitz. You may be curious about their earlier work, about their working situation and their relationship with other artists, and you may read about them in the libarary. This will help to enrich your understanding; but first of all, learn to know the sculpture itself.

52 *Child's path from home to school.*

13

Experiments in Response
to Line Quality

The difference between seeing a line as a static, accomplished fact and seeing it as the movement of a point is the difference between seeing product and seeing process. The educator knows that difference as it exists in the well-mapped route of the lesson plan compared to the moving "point" of the individual's attention and learning. The line of the route may be planned to predict not only the direction of the learning's content but also its extent and its steps, leaving open mainly the question of speed and travel time. But the classroom teacher knows the special ways by which the individual child recreates that lesson plan route in his own unique terms and realizes himself in the moving.

The quality of lineness or linearity is so integral a part of the sequential movement and continuity of life experience that we ordinarily take it for granted. The end result of moving is usually thought of simply as accomplished distance.

Growing infants review for us some of the varied processes of locomotion, to be forgotten later and replaced by such abstractions as "line *AB*" or the time-rate formula for measuring its traversal. The purposeful directness of *AB* takes us across the floor to a favorite toy or through space to the moon, while another purpose, like hunting mushrooms or wild flowers, might take us on a stop/go, zigzag trail through the woods. The improvised paths of strolling, wandering, and "just looking around" are relaxed and informal compared to the hopping, skipping, strutting or leaping which forget *A* and *B* in celebration of movement itself.

Out of all our experiences in moving, we store an understanding of such linear differences as goal bound *vs.* improvised, plodding *vs.* soaring, timid *vs.* aggressive, monotonous *vs.* varied, broken *vs.* continuous, and so on; but the feeling aspect of movement experience is rich—too rich to sort into neat classifications.

The qualities experienced bodily in locomotion are reflected in all of our movements, including those of hands and eyes. A light attached to the hand of the fencer or the machine operator records on film a trail of purposeful skill. From stadium sidelines, we soar with the ball and bounce and roll to a stop with it. Picasso, photographed through the glass he is painting on, moves to reveal to us his vision in evolution.

With the internalized experience of our own movement, we respond to qualitative differences in the observed movement of other people and things and in the movement recorded or implied in line. Actually, the difference between line as observed movement and as recorded movement is the difference between specified and unspecified time, rate, and direction. Thus we see the curve in floor pattern inscribed by the swiftly moving dancer and the similar sweep of brush stroke in a painting. In one, the moving dancer conducts our eyes along the curve, and in the other, the curve, as it exists in the painting, draws our eyes along it—fast, slow, perhaps in one direction, perhaps in another—within the interplay of the whole composition. Both in the "time arts" (dance, music, literature, drama, cinema) and the "non-time" arts (drawing, painting, sculpture, architecture, industrial design), the observer participates by "going with" their linear aspects; but this participation differs greatly in complexity. For example, anyone who has skated figure eights will recall the feeling of swinging around one center, then smoothly, gradually leaving it to turn back around another. It is like a steady flow alternating around two gravitational fields. By contrast, the figure eight trail itself, as a static, visualized object, invites many other associations, such as a pair of symmetrical, centralized regions, each extending minimum contact to the other, or, more likely, as a double loop track with a crackup crossroads or intersection in the middle. If the eye is stopped by the X of that crossing, the continuous flowing of the curves is interrupted; so, if one were trying to capture in a drawing the hypnotic feeling of endless, flowing movement which one experiences in skating figure eights, he would have to work with the flowing lines until *they* evoked the right feeling, whether they looked like a figure eight or not.*

---

*This process of "giving form to feeling" differentiates art expression from simply venting one's feelings, according to Susanne K. Langer. See her "Problems of Form," Chapter 2.

Experiments With Line in Two Dimensions

Experiment 21A:

Drawing Linear Movement

Using a piece of soft black chalk, charcoal, or crayon, draw large, free-swinging lines clear across big sheets of newsprint or the want ad pages of a newspaper. Stand to give yourself more freedom of movement. Draw different kinds of moving lines, such as purposeful, hunting-around, soaring, staggering, wandering, charging, jittering, tiptoeing, undulating, etc. Let them cross and cover each other. Fill several sheets with them. What you are observing is the expressive character of individual linear movement.

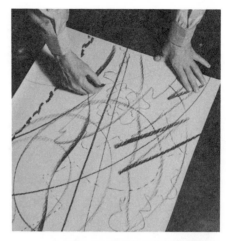

53 *A point moving in many ways.*

Experiment 21B:

Line Quality as Edges

Looking over the scribbled sheets, pick out some of the paths which seem to express most clearly a certain quality, character, or feeling of movement and label each with a penciled word to describe that quality. Finally take scissors and cut along one of these expressive lines, making it the outline or edge of a paper shape. Place the cut sheet against a dark wall or floor and see how the linear movement is now expressed by the cut edge. Compare this with linear quality of a torn edge.

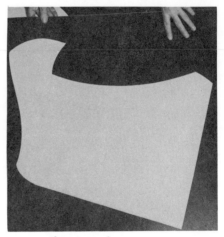

54 *Along cut edges . . .*

56 *. . . and broken edges.*

55 *Line quality in torn edges . . .*

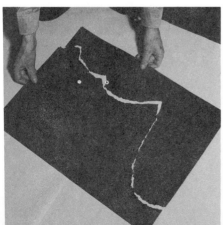

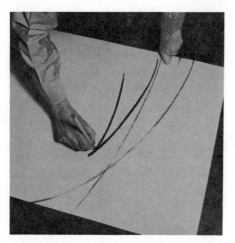

57   *Discover how a brush can move.*

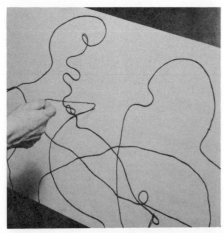

58   *Continuity with changes.*

59   *Crossings.*

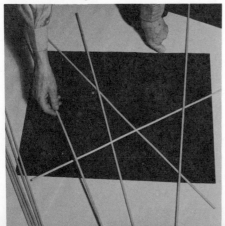

Experiment 21C:
Relating Linear Strokes

After observing single lines, try to relate them. This could be done with the same drawing instrument used earlier or you could change to ink and a brush, such as one of the bamboo-handled Japanese writing tools. (Everybody should have the experience of working with one of these brushes!) With some practice you will be able to vary the width and sweep of your strokes so they express a range of dynamics—heavy *vs.* light, fast *vs.* slow, sleek *vs.* spluttery, and so on.

On the blank surface of a large sheet of newsprint, move out one of the kinds of expressive lines you made earlier. Then ask yourself what kind of linear movement would work with that line, to act as a sort of companion or associate, but not to dominate or detract from it. After you have added such a line, you may wish to include another, or several others, all working *with* the original movement. If they become so harmonious that they are boring, try a contrasting or opposing line. The question in these studies is how expressive lines are modified by other associated lines.

Experiment 21D:
Continuing, Flowing Line

From our earlier work with found materials we know that a length of string, dampened, and contrasting in color with the paper, can be lowered carefully onto paper on the floor. Not wishing to make anything, we are producing line patterns which can be studied as they are being formed.

Experiment 21E:
Straight Lines Interact

Similar study can be given the straight lines of dowel sticks or bamboo garden stakes arranged on a sheet of paper on the floor.

Experiment 22:

Photographing a Light Trail

An interesting method of moving a point to produce a line on a two-dimensional surface is to record it on photosensitive film or paper in the way trails of head-lights are recorded in night photography. This method requires a darkened room, one or two flashlights, and a camera which can be set for time exposures. The camera, on a tripod or table, is focused on a large, open floor space in a dark room and with the shutter opened. A dancer (yourself) turns on a flashlight and keeps it pointed toward the camera, moving it steadily, smoothly in curves and straight lines, high, low, and across the confines of the space. The light may be turned off, moved, and turned on again.

The linear track of the light will be inscribed on the film (see Figure 60). The special advantage of this experiment in line is that it uses large, dancelike movements, involving the sweep and thrust of the whole body as it moves with the light.

Experiment 23:

Line in Three Dimensions

The photographic record of the flashlight's trail reduces to a two-dimensional surface what was really a flight in three-dimensional space. Had the camera "seen" it from another angle, it would have captured an entirely different image—one perhaps more, perhaps less expressive of the movement itself.

60   *Trails of a dancing flashlight.*

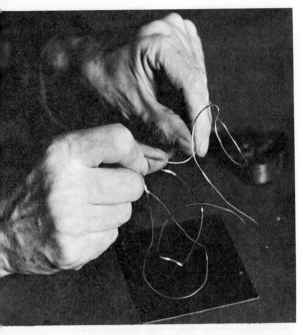

61   *Flight line in space.*

62   *Body size linear movement.*

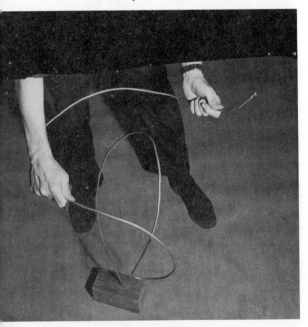

In order to study linear movement in three dimensions, we need to find a manageable linelike stuff with which to work. If there were no air movements to disturb them, the vapor trails of jet planes would provide working materials on a heroic scale. More accessible and controllable linear media are metal rods and wires, rigid for permanent sculptural products, but yielding and responsive for our manipulation and study.*

For work on a small scale, the best wire for line study is soft copper, aluminum, or annealed (not tempered) iron wire. Solid wire solder also works well, but its lead content makes prolonged handling unsafe. Art stores sell aluminum armature wire, one-eighth or three-sixteenths of an inch in diameter, for sculptors' armatures. This heavy but soft wire allows you to work on a scale large enough so that the movements in the wire are easily related to your own body movements and gestures.

In estimating the length of wire needed, having too little is usually better than too much. The length is used without adding other pieces and usually without additional cutting. Using the heavier armature wire, flight patterns several feet high may develop, requiring a total length of six or seven feet. Because the finer copper or iron wire is suited to constructions less than a foot tall, thirty to thirty-six inches will be enough.

A base for one's sculpture is desirable. Young children sometimes use a ball of clay or a piece of styrofoam to stick wire (and other stiff, linear things) into, but a heavy, pre-drilled wooden block will probably work better for large constructions; smaller blocks or cardboard bases are good for working with finer wire. Since our purpose is to study how lines move in space rather than to produce independent sculptural objects, we need bases which only hold our wire lines in working position and add a minimum of visual distraction. Later work with wire may omit bases altogether.

---

*Pipe cleaners are easily fashioned but are too short and textural. Straightened coat hangers have a springy stiffness which is sometimes useful but poorly suited to our present purposes. Reed is another useful kind of line material but it insists stubbornly on its own looping character.

First straighten out the length of wire, using hand and thumb pressure and learning to view its line from more than one side. Usually work begins with one end of the wire, perhaps inserted in a base. (If the other end is whipping about, it is safer, especially for children, to cap it with a small piece of masking tape.)

Working with wire, as with any medium, gradually brings awareness of the special qualities of the stuff itself and how it needs to be worked with. It has much of the changeable suggestibility of clay and can be "smoothed out to start over" by pulling its length back and forth over a rounded pipe or chair leg.

Start the line's movement by departing from base, floor, or table, shooting upward or outward in straight, curving, or zigzag flight, then curving or turning, gradually or suddenly, in other directions, entering and inscribing new spatial volumes as you develop the character of a lineal movement. Most important, keep turning the work or walking around it so that you are seeing and working with three-dimensional lines in space, not with any two-dimensional view; look at it not only from its sides but from above, below, and any vantage point which will help make clear how the line is moving.

63   *To begin again.*

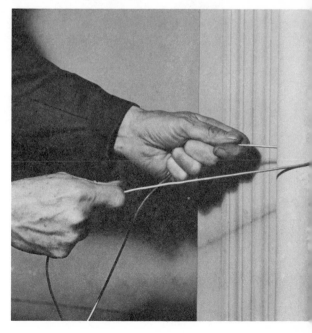

In order to work with a line, one must move with it. The usual way of moving only one's eyes along the line is less helpful than "moving the line" with hand, arm, torso, or entire body, as well as with eyes, and knowing from the feeling of the moving whether the sequence of directions, speeds, durations, slight and vigorous changes, makes sense or needs revision. It is also necessary to view the cumulative, visual whole to avoid confusion of contradictory overlays of movement. Thus, the conflicts and "traffic jams" which may appear in some views of the wire will need to be opened up, separated, or otherwise made more simple and clear.

The simplicity of a brief lyrical statement is best suited to such single line composing with wire, but its movement need not be confined to the curves of gliding or soaring. The fact that wire is usually presented to us in the circles and spirals of coils tends to limit first expressions with it to a looping kind of Spencerian writing exercise; but we know movement can dart, dodge, turn, and reverse as well as swing and swoop. Small linear beginnings can step and struggle toward a climax and then zoom for home.

Observing Related Movements

In football the question about a forward pass is whether the moving ball and a moving receiver will meet or be blocked by still other moving elements. In such logistics the individual linear movements draw their meaning from a certain relationship in time and space—witness moon shots! Meaning of a different kind may come from changing relationships between lines of voices in music* or paths of movement in dance as they approach, clash, depart, follow, come to rest, and so on. In visual arts these virtual lines, the paths or trails of implied motion, are part of our rising with the verticals of the cathedral or swinging between the reds of a painting or watching the infinite changes within a mobile.**

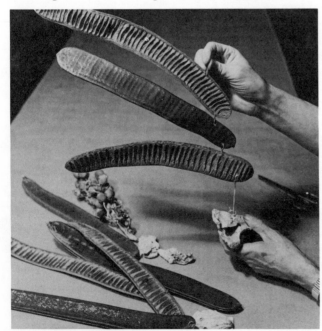

64   *Sails for moving.*

*For example, Bartok's *Mikrokosmos,* recorded by Mace, #M9007.
**Appendix, pp. 199, suggesting experiments with mobiles.

14

Experiments in Seeing and Saying:
Creating an Image

Much of our learning is directed toward seeing things "as they are" in order to estimate possibilities for change. In the process of problem solving we need an accurate, objective assessment of present conditions, and, to check against the distortion of personal experience, we ask others, in effect, "Do you see what I see?" Instruments like the camera and the electric eye are taking over these tasks, but no doubt we shall always need rigorously impersonal seeing for scientific observation and verification.

Aesthetic experience and creative work require, at least in the essential discovery stages, a different kind of seeing. Instead of maintaining our distance from the object, we identify with it, we intuitively feel our way into it, we see it "from inside."

Lest we assume that these contrasting ways of seeing are automatically associated with science on the one hand and with art on the other, we should note that through such visual aids as television and picture magazines millions "see" many examples of both kinds of images with little apparent personal response beyond, "What else is new?" What we need, as individuals and as a society, is to identify ourselves generously with something outside ourselves and to learn to see with concern, whether it is the concern of the scientist or the concern of the artist.

Our skills in visual communication have leap-frogged forward as a part of the elaborate technology of merchandising. We approach the time when, if we will just relax, we can see anything, introduced by the proper "motivation" and conceptually packaged; our reactions to it are analyzed and even measured. With the increasing interest of industry in the large-scale production of educational equipment, educators have a critical responsibility to be clear, and to make clear, what it means to *see*.

We have watched infants selecting out of a buzzing confusion not only the bright, lighted, and moving objects but also those which promise the most satisfaction to their immediate needs. With experience, children see with increased individuality. The achievement of deep involvement probably depends more on the individual's internal organization than on the external conditions of visual perception, for one must exist confidently as a person before he can give himself to this or any relationship.

Why do we go beyond the intuitive identification of aesthetic seeing to *say* what it is that we see? There is increasing agreement among biologists and psychologists that the urge to say, to assert, and to form is a part of normal human development.*

65   *Image maker.*

---

*See E. G. Schactel, *Metamorphosis: On the Development of Affect, Perception, Attention and Memory.* New York: Basic Books, 1959, pp. 241-242.

Out of our feeling of being part of something, it seems natural for us to say how it is. Such a statement may bring varying degrees of satisfaction to the "sayer," perhaps by its feeling of rightness, but more often through the answering response of others. These degrees of satisfaction, resulting from many expressive ventures, become the batting average with which we face new situations of seeing and saying. However, most of us have at some point stopped taking chances with certain kinds of personally expressive statement, such as dancing, drawing, or singing, because they failed to offer us the satisfaction of shared experience. Everybody's figure of a man, for example, like everybody's letter B or everybody's proverb, probably seemed much more negotiable currency for the social transactions of seeing and saying.

Most of our experiments in previous chapters have dealt with selected aesthetic factors, such as texture, color, or three-dimensional organization, in deliberate separation from the complicated matrix of real things. To help us adults take fresh hold on such aesthetic qualities in the world around us, we had to avoid the usual handles of recognizable identity, such as name, source, use, or common value of objects and object relationships in reality. But identifying ourselves closely with the reality of our environment (both external and internal) is a main source of aesthetic experience, and the quality of involvement in that identification is what leads to the creation of freshly seen, evocative images.

The process of forming images of things we experience can demand the devotion of a lifetime, but it can also be sampled on a very simple scale.

Experiment 24:

Creating a Visual Image of a Familiar Object

We think of drawing skill as requiring long practice, and that is true; but it is possible for any of us to use what skill we have to create a visual image of something we are used to seeing.

As a suggestion, reach into your pockets or handbag and take out the clutter of familiar items which you carry around with you. One of these things should be suitable for an experiment in image making, using charcoal and rough, cheap paper about 12 by 18 inches or larger. Select some object whose shape or other visual quality appeals to you as being interesting and not too complicated. If there are elaborate patterns of printing, writing, or illustration on it, you can omit them unless they have some special visual interest to you. The object may be hard and formal, or wrinkled, worn and informal.

Before you begin drawing, study the object attentively and patiently. Handle it, turn it, and look into and along and around it until you begin to see in it a kind of wholeness within which parts or features exist, but which is a complete world in itself. Then notice how that whole thing goes, moves, reaches out this way, curves around in that way. In short, see what constitutes its main visual character.

Using your moving hand, without the charcoal, "draw" the way it goes across the large, empty sheet. Now draw it in with charcoal, as large as possible. Keep your lines free and perhaps light at first, but sooner or later outline firmly what you have seen, bringing out especially those characteristics you noted.

Lean your drawing against something and study it from six or eight feet away. Look for the ways in which it begins to show the special expressive character which the object has suggested to you. Try not to let questions of objective "correctness," such as accuracy of proportions, take precedence over the personal selection and interpretation of your own image. What you are saying is how it is to you, not how it would be to everybody.

66   *Look until you begin to see it.*

It may help you to put the original object aside at some point as the working conditions change, for now, of

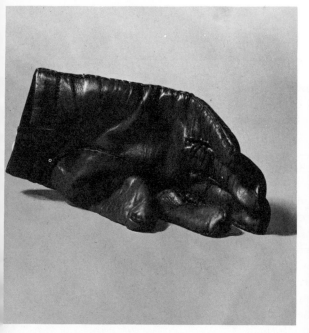

course, there is a new object appearing—your drawing. It will begin to embody your seeing, but it will also take on a life of its own as you work with it. In other words, your drawing may set up its own demands as to how your vision will live in it. For example, you might find that light shading, toning, or smudging would help show planes within the image. Then stronger shading, or even an added chalk color, might be needed behind or around the object to give definition to the whole and to make it sit better in the drawing's space.

Since your purpose is to study the process of creating a visual image through intuitive identification with an environmental object, you need not be too concerned if, in working on the drawing, you carry it too far and lose or spoil it as an independent product. The main test of your image is whether it suggests to you the quality you saw. It might also reveal the object in a new and vivid way to others; such an effect is more likely as you gain assurance in this kind of seeing and saying.

It is important to apply the process of forming an image to different kinds of objects, such as something which suggests a history of use—an old glove, a crumpled paper—or something which bears within it the unity of natural growth, such as a flower, vegetable, fruit, or even your finger or hand. In earlier chapters on three-

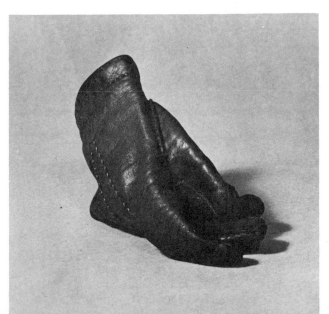

dimensional form and space, experiments in observing were clarified and reinforced by insistent scribbles to indicate the main visual character which had been observed.

All of these experiments in creating visual images depend more on seeing eyes than on facile crayons or pencils, but the act of committing the image to paper distills and strengthens the seeing.*

---

*For a more thorough discussion of developing seeing with specific drawing processes, see *The Natural Way to Draw*, by Kimon Nicolaides.

67   *The right to see and say.*

Image Making in Different Situations

Teachers know how functional situations affect seeing and saying. They understand, for example, that the image a child makes of a pet would probably be influenced by the presence in the working environment of the pet itself, of others' representations of it, or of a demonstration of how to do it. Teachers might also understand that the actual effect of these external factors depends on the child's internalized experience, including the sum of his past ventures in image making. They might know that the child's aesthetic/creative response to any experience would depend partly on his assurance of his right to see and react to it in his own way. In reality image making usually takes place surrounded by predetermined images, present or

68   *The best ideas of all members.*

remembered, so that if one is to maintain individuality of expression, some reassurance of one's right to it may be needed.

Opportunities for open-ended developments vary greatly. Most of the experiments described in this book have been designed to encourage individual response to perceptual materials. The content of these experiences grew out of interplay between sensory involvement and the thinking/feeling associations evoked. However, the process sometimes starts with thinking/feeling content and seeks sensory means to give it form. Thus the assigned topics of much school art work must include a self-assigned feeling content if aesthetic image making is to develop.*

Some working processes, such as those described in the puppetry and the found sounds experiments, involve several people sharing ideas and developing an image together. The extent to which such cooperation can achieve the quality of aesthetic experience and creative work, which are essentially individual processes, depends on many social and psychological factors.** These cannot be discussed here except to note the need for involvement which would permit, invite, and even demand the best ideas of all members, rather than those which are most accessible, acceptable, or communicable. The importance of incorporating depth of feeling and thinking experience into the planning and working of face-to-face groups suggests the need for much more sensitive interaction and for whatever will encourage it.

Expressing Images in Different Media

Drawing is a more expressive medium than many of us think, and it is good to see new interest in restoring it to the use of the nonspecialist. However, when describing vivid personal experience, other media, especially body movement and gesture, usually take precedence over drawing. In all its variations, from inside tensing/relaxing to changing posture and sweeping gesture, body sensing has been a primary means of identification with the original experience, and it is a natural means of expressing what happened.

The whole body expression of a child bursting to tell what he has experienced is well known to the teacher, who may help by inviting the child to "show us." For most adults such invitations have long been countered by, "Don't point," and "Sit still and listen," until, if our bodily saying is to be read at all, it must be done by lip reading. But experimenting will still help us to become aware of body movement as a means of personal expression.

---

*See the Appendix, p. 197, "Criteria for Planning Creative Art Projects Which Are Related to Other Curriculum Areas."

**See the author's "Creative Work within a Group: Its Situational Factors," in *Research in Art Education*. NAEA, 9th Yearbook, 1959, pp. 45-51.

Experiment 25:

Expression Through Body Movement

Try to give bodily expression to some vivid aesthetic experience, not in the form of charades or pantomimed storytelling, but as the expressive image of certain qualitative states or relationships: how it was, for example, in some outstanding experience with a place, a sound, or a person. Of course, you would need to start with an experience of your own choosing, since expressive images are given, not assigned or taken. Let your head, your shoulders, your whole body enter into the expression, even if there is little moving which might be visible to others. Imagine that you are trying to communicate to friends who speak a different language some vivid experience, such as the approach of flood waters, the head of the parade, or the first peeking out of springtime.

Of the media used in creating expressive images, words can be among the most evocative. Especially in speech, with its rich coloration and spacing, one can reveal the quality of experience to a listener. Our playwrights know the power of even the most common words and timeworn expressions when they are uttered in the context of feeling. But when words are cut off from the speaker's presence, they must be chosen well to convey the immediacy of aesthetic experience. The problem is exemplified by most letter writing, which would be flat and uncommunicative if we could not read into the poor words the imagined presence of the writer.

We can, however, recall poetic images which bring a direct sensing of reality—we are there!—and sometimes an insight into the full significance of that reality. This may be accomplished through metaphors and other figures of speech, provided they are won by the same process of intuitive identification with the object (being with it, in it, of it) which we have been using in creating visual images.

Young children and poets provide examples:

> The rain screws up its face
> And falls to bits.
> Then it makes itself again.
> Only the rain can make itself again.
>
> *New Zealand Boy*, age 4
> *in "Miracles"**

Miracles: Poems by Children of the English Speaking World, collected by Richard Lewis. New York: Simon and Schuster, 1966.

I . . . saw the ruddy moon lean over a hedge
Like a red-faced farmer,
    . . . and round about were the wistful stars
With white faces like town children

                 T. E. Hulme
                 "Autumn"

The birds have all flown
And I am alone
In the big sky's mouth.

                 American Boy. age 10

It was midnight
The sky was dark black
The stars were threepenny bits
The Sea was making a sound
Like a silk dress.

                 Australian girl, age 8
                 in "Miracles"*

Experiment 26:

Wording a Poetic Image

Without being too ambitious, try to word a brief statement about some simple thing which you have experienced deeply, to see if you can say how it felt rather than objectively talking *about* it. It may be a response to a quality in an object or a friend; it may be part of your day's activity, a special place, a change, a reckoning, or any of many moments of insight or revelation.

*Ibid.

Examples of efforts by amateur adults are:

> A strawberry soda
> With a red brown mane.
> Well-creased boys with half smiles.

Try writing several of these poetic images, and test them by asking yourself whether they present your experience freshly and vividly.

Experiment 27:

Observing Juxtaposition of Images

Present day images are rarely simple, unqualified statements, and least of all when they purport to be. Today we may feel the peroration *needs* the kitten rubbing against the orator's legs, the bronze warrior *needs* the perching pigeon, and so on, because the combination may be truer to our feelings of rightness than is the isolated image. Movie directors make outstanding use of this juxtaposition of images. Thus we see the things in the shop window, but we also see the reflecting of ourselves, seeing—and perhaps wanting. The important image is the image of relationship, because it is in relationship that nuances of feeling are revealed.

Check this with your own experience by noticing examples of straightforward, everyday images which take on special meaning only from their occurrence in interesting, unexpected combination.

Most people find that certain media seem especially suitable for expressing certain kinds of images. But each person sees such relationships in his own unique way, and to generalize them would be unintelligible to the rest of us. The loss of most of our meaning in verbal communication is often ascribed to the inadequacy of our words or listening since speech is, for most of us, the main medium for image making. Gaining access to other satisfying media would no doubt enrich our seeing and saying. But meaningful images arise more from a deep involvement in aesthetic experience than from facility with media. Mixed media have assumed importance in all of the arts because of the increasing complexity of our poetic images, not because of interest in novel mixtures.

We have been examining the creation of images as a means of clarifying aesthetic experience. Individuals have the right and also the responsibility to enter generously into the acts of seeing and saying, for through processes of intuitive identification and invention they can contribute to life-giving, creative possibilities for their fellows.

15

Experiments in Response to Interaction of Color

Most of us adults have been exposed to some scientific explanation of color analysis and perception; and many of us, in our work, go on to master at least some part of a growing color technology.

As teachers, we observe how color materials attract children's interest and curiosity, bringing pleasure to their visual inventing as well as leading them on into questions and experiments in optics and physics. For example, watching the family's eighteen-month-old toddler pull *only* red books out of the shelves makes us wonder when he will be attracted to violet. Indeed, for both adults and children, work with color should offer unusual opportunity for combining the personal sensing and expression of art with the more impersonal theory and analysis of science. How the eye sees color and how colors work, in pigment and in light, are so teachable with exciting experiments, attractive visual aids and reading, that helping children to develop their own personal response to color is often neglected. On the other hand, children's early introduction to the time-honored color wheel has been widely questioned in recent years. It had become a deadening departure from personal response, in favor of generally demonstrable information and rules for tastelessly correct color schemes. School policy on teaching color illustrates the need for clear insights into how we learn *aesthetically* as well as scientifically.

In Chapter 8 we noted that color is a major reason why many found stuffs are chosen for creative work in collage. When color is the main concern, variables such as texture should be limited.

Anyone who has not yet worked in collage with the found materials of colored paper will find it an excellent introduction to color interaction. The possibility of ready rearrangement makes collage especially suited for such study; and even though available color materials may be limited, one has a wealth of possibilities in deciding "How much?" and "Where?" However, we should try to improve the range and quality of our collage colors, instead of remaining satisfied with whatever comes to hand.

Experiment 28:

Paper Collage of Found Printed Color

Pieces of colored paper, in a palette far richer than school construction papers offer, can be clipped out of colored advertisements and illustrations in old magazines and sorted into separate piles or folders of colors. In selecting color areas to cut out, look for uniformity of color regardless of the pictured objects.* While the "stuff" is only ink on paper, your found material here is color, along with a variety of represented textures and tonal gradations. The addition of some solid color papers such as coated or poster papers will enrich your color collage resources.

Working on a neutral background paper (black, white, or gray) gives the colors you add the best chance to speak for themselves. Since most of the cut pieces of color will be small and you will probably cover the background, try to limit its size to twelve by eighteen

---

*Taking one's color materials from pictured objects and working with these materials simply as color means bypassing the chance to put together the various meanings associated with the represented objects themselves. This elimination of "content" or object-centered meaning might offer difficulties to many adults for whom color has become a poor second to shape in a recognizable world, but it can also refresh their awareness of color. On the other hand, for a child struggling to attach names to thing/images, such abstraction would probably be distracting. It would be better for him, for example, to get the color for his pumpkin from a piece of colored construction paper than from a large picture of an orange.

inches or smaller. In order to avoid distracting your attention from relating the colors, it may help to tear rather than cut the printed color papers, so that shaping does not take its usual precedence. The torn edges may add an interesting, irregular white line to your visual materials.

In any one of your families of clipped colors you will probably find a great variety of tints and shades, ranging from subtle to strong. Try setting up a passage or sequence of these variations, laying color beside color on the background sheet until you have established a kind of color situation there, among interacting blues, for example. You may then wish to extend, repeat, or vary this, beginning elsewhere in the space, or you may need different colors. As you work you will find that colors (not shapes) are leading your eyes from one part to another, more or less strongly. Thus you may move down through a series of reds along the left but remain aware of that other little red peeking out at the right. If your eyes are being led out of the space, as at the corners, try revising and shifting the color arrangements to keep the action inside, without losing the informal variety of movement.

Sometimes study of the whole collage is made easier by laying it on the floor to increase your distance from it. Whether you will wish to fasten your color swatches will depend on whether you want to hang it up for further study.

Experiment 29:

Colored Tissue Collage

Assorted colored tissue papers, available in art and school supply stores, have enriched, because of their transparency, our range of color choices for paper collage work. Again, set up separate folders for each family of colors, to include both uncut pieces and leftovers. Work on a white background, not too large, of cardboard or heavy paper. Use liquid starch or other watered-down paste, applied freely with a brush. The fact that the colors will "bleed" somewhat will encourage overlay of torn strips and pieces rather than precisely cut picture-making in isolated colors. Work fairly rapidly, paying attention to the whole composition. The buildup of combined colors can be rich and exciting. Incidentally, to avoid later curling of the background sheet, paste newsprint on its back surface.

Working with these tissues shows that, no matter what our experience, clear and attractive color materials are an asset, for usually our pleasure in these straight-color beginnings leads us on into continued work. Before long we find a challenge in coordinating the changed colors of the wet papers in over-all relationships which seem just right to us. This may mean working out a satisfying space relationship of limited color intervals: limited, that is, in the number of colors included, in the range of dark and light, or in brightness.

Experiment 30:

Color in "Colorless" Collage

Exploiting color limitations suggests an experiment in "colorless" collage, composed of sheet materials of various fibers, to which no pigments or dyes have been added. For example, most households would yield a wide variety of "colorless" papers: tissues, cardboards, napkins, towels, wax paper, packing and wrapping papers, and so on. Or you could choose wood fibers, shavings, saw dust, sand, shells, and weeds, or undyed fibers of cotton, hemp, wool, and silk.

Working with these materials becomes exciting precisely because what was chosen as colorless turns out to give a lovely play of subtle color differences—not the bright differences of a brass band, to be sure, but the closer relationships of a string quartet, perhaps.

Experiment 31:

Color Modifications with Paints

To face the challenge of working with a full range of color differences, we would need either an infinite choice of color materials, as in our papers or in the many yarn colors of the tapestry weaver, or we would need to be able to modify the coloring media themselves, as in paints, dyes, or light.

Children are usually experienced picture makers before they become interested in deliberate color mixing and control; but as adults we can work with color more freely if we stay away from picture making, with its plans and outlines, to simply make and relate improvised areas of colors.

If you have not had the experience of mixing paints so that you can produce *any color you wish,* you should try it. The ability to modify paint color at will by combining color ingredients will improve not only your skill in painting, but even more, your seeing of color differences in the world around you.

Materials and procedures for painting are discussed fully in many books, so we shall limit our discussion to the simplest essentials for our experimenting. In color theory, it should be sufficient to recall, and then to try out, the three dimensions of color differences:

1. *Hue,* meaning color, such as yellow or yellow/ orange. All hues are derived from the primary colors, red, yellow, and blue.
2. *Value,* meaning lightness ("high" value), or darkness ("low" value) as from an almost-white blue to an almost-black blue.
3. *Intensity,* or saturation, meaning strength or brightness, as from the brightest possible green to a "softened" green approaching neutral gray.

Working with paints often reveals a gap between color theory and practice, when color problems must be solved with less than perfect materials. Probably the easiest paints for us to experiment with are tempera or poster paints, the opaque colors used by school children. You will need the primary colors, red, yellow, and blue, plus black and white. These colors are often too impure to enable you to mix all other colors. For instance, the red

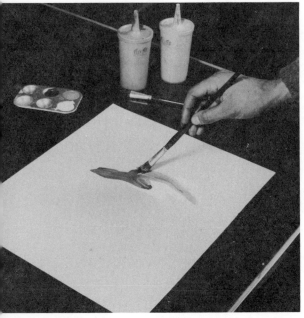

69   *A workable setup for painting experiment.*

70   *Another workable setup.*

may contain some yellow, and will not mix with blue to make a clear violet. Thus you may find it helps to have two reds: a vermilion and a magenta; and two blues: an ultramarine and a turquoise. You will probably find that you use more white than any other color. Use small amounts of several colors in a muffin tin kind of pallet (see Figure 69); have a large can of water with a damp sponge nearby for wiping your brush, one or two ½″ to ¾″ bristle easel brushes, such as children use, small pieces of sponge, and a supply of 18″ by 24″ newsprint. Most of these supplies are standard for young children. Instead of an easel you can use a washable table top and stand as you work.

An interesting way to improve your color skill is to make many variations of one color; for example, mix a half dozen different (dark/light) *values* of one hue, such as a red/orange. With these opaque paints, lighter *tints* are produced by adding white, and darker *shades* by adding black. A common mistake is to add both black and white to a color, thus muffling and weakening its color character.

Next, try mixing several different *intensities* of one color, perhaps making them all of approximately the same dark/light value. To reduce the intensity or brightness of a color you will need to add a little of the primary color (or colors) not already in the color. For example, to soften a green, which contains blue and yellow, you would add a trace of the missing red. Or to soften a blue, you would add both red and yellow.

You can probably mix the colors right on the paper while they are still wet. For more leisurely mixing use an old dinner plate as a pallet. If you paint a fairly generous sample of each of your values and intensities of a color, it will later be interesting to organize a collage out of the color materials you have made. However, it is not necessary to turn out dutiful rows of color swatches. While you are working, you might as well paint large and small informal areas of color, shaping and placing them as you please. Afterwards you can check to see what range of values and intensities you have included in your improvised arrangements.

This concentration on modifying colors in terms of each of the three dimensions and then in combinations of them will enable you not only to distinguish more differences between colors, as in dress materials, but also to know of what these differences consist. For example, try analyzing some of the colors you find about you, including some of the more complex natural colors, such as wood, leather, or stone. Putting aside questions of texture and light reflection, ask yourself just what color it is, what light-to-dark value it is, and what strong-to-neutral intensity it is. Next, state what paint colors you would use to make that color, in what priority and order, and in what amounts. (Simply listing ingredients would not mean much since most natural colors include all of the primary colors.) Your experience in color mixing will warn you about making theoretical estimates without regard for the idiosyncracies of the pigments with which you are working. For instance, wet tempera colors usually turn lighter as they dry. To test your analyzing, try mixing a few colors to see how they match an observed color, such as a book cover or the floor.

Such exercises may seem far removed from the personally expressive spontaneity we associate with art work, and indeed, if skills in color matching were being demanded or imposed as ends in themselves, they could reduce the aesthetic experiencing of colors to mere skill training. However, some self-assigned perfecting of skills, whether in making or in finding, is a necessary part of creative work and is observed as a natural part of children's growing up. Because we adults sometimes take refuge in the security of such exercises, and in the test scores which may accompany them, it will usually be better for us to subordinate them to personal invention and sensuous play.

Experiment 32:

Painting Improvised Color Arrangements

By now you know that a good range of paint colors may be needed to work with even one color. To make an "all blue" painting, for example, might require red and yellow (to reduce the blue's intensity) and black and white (to change its value). Equipped with such variety of colors and standing so that your eyes can include the whole paper as you work on any part of it, begin by simply laying on, somewhere, an unshaped area of any

color you like. Then select or make a color to go with it and add it, nearby or elsewhere, noting any effect of the relationship. Sometimes colors begin to take on a kind of positive "presence" as you see them existing together in the space; and combining this with half-seen possibilities will suggest the next colors. They may be similar to the colors present or different in hue, value, or intensity, as well as in amount and placement. As in a conversation among friends, it is generally better to let one thing lead to another than constantly to change the subject, but most important is to pay attention to what goes on and to participate in it. Color themes and variations will develop more by hunch than by plan or convention. The more you become involved in the color action, the more your hunches will take on the responsible confidence expressed by, "That feels right to me."

71 *Looking at colors through a "Finder."*

72 *Studying the interplay of colors.*

Even though the purpose of this painting experiment is to study color rather than to make paintings, there are advantages in staying with a "color situation" in order to see some of the possibilities for evocative statement in colors working together beyond the beginning stages. Because tempera paints are opaque, you can paint or repaint over dry sections that may need reorganizing or simplifying.

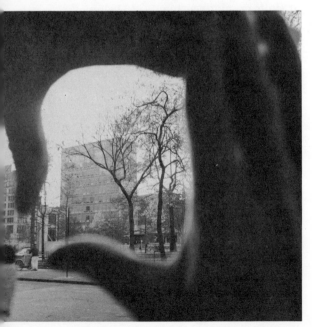

Note what kinds of questions seem to help you move on into your study of color. You may find, for example, that simply looking at your work from a distance of a few feet is the best way to ask yourself, "What next?" Questionable color relationships can be tested by temporarily blocking them out with your hand while viewing the whole. Some parts may seem separate, not working, or distracting. Experience will bring you an effective, personal array of such working questions. Of course, they do not imply that you are trying to get all parts of your painting to live together in some bland kind of harmony; that is how the paper was before you began! Instead, your questions should guide and clarify the new color action which you are developing.

Experiment 33:

Looking for Environmental Color Relationships

Your work in constructing and modifying color relationships with paints will be enriched and extended if it is accompanied by a hunt for interesting color combinations in your surroundings. You can do this by blocking out the peripheral field of vision, using your hands or a black paper frame to serve as a cameralike "finder," so that you can focus on a limited grouping of adjacent colors. Again, try to discount all stuff characteristics except color. From your color mixing experience you may note where color elements are shared and to what extent; you may observe differences in brightness and in dark/light values; two colors may appear in close harmony but in strong contrast with a third color. Shift your finder frame and your own position to adjust quantities and proportions of colors included until you feel, "That's it!"

Studying Color in Works of Art

Looking for colors in the open environment means that you both find them and relate them. It is a very different experience to study color relationships in the paintings, tapestries, mosaics, stained glass, and other works by masters of color.

The process of looking at color in a work of art is not one of analytical measuring of separate elements or of applying laws of composition. It is more like entering into the life of a special universe or color system which has its own laws and its own consistent relationships. Knowing other works by the same artist may hasten the process of knowing "how it is," but each work is a new entity to be participated in on its own terms, including the behavior of its color.

Such study is greatly enhanced by having access to original works of art, with enough time to really work with them. When you know how refreshing the viewing of art can be, the next steps are to learn what art is available and to work this viewing into your regular routine. It is remarkable, for example, how many city dwellers are including brief gallery visits in their noon-hour schedule. The hours you spend with works of great quality provide an important extension of your aesthetic experiencing in color, even when color is not, in itself, the artist's first concern; and it is also true that your own ventures in making, modifying, and discovering color relationships can help you to see, enjoy, and take a more active part in the interplay of colors provided by a master.

16

Experiments in Color Sequence

There is a time factor in responding to any interplay of color, whether in a painting or in the successive movements of a dance. In visual priorities and in duration and direction of eye movement, most paintings leave much freedom to the viewer, although exhibits, typographical layout, architecture, and sculpture may control the time order of these visual responses to a greater degree. But responding to sequences of color in a specified time dimension is a different aesthetic experience and a point of increasing interest in the arts.

Experiment 34:

Choreographed Color Collage

Chapter 10 described experiments in choreographing collage within the proscenium of a puppet stage. The materials and lights used in this work may emphasize color as one of many factors in the developing sequence suggested by the music. Omitting the music and working only with materials chosen for their color—cloth, paper, cardboard, and on occasion, colored light—would focus one's work on composing with color and time.

On a larger scale, color, either worn as costumes or, preferably, carried as scarves or panels, can be moved by a group of amateur dancers. This work requires a collection of pieces of cloth, from one to several yards in length and including a good range of solid colors. Groups of six to eight members work best. Since the "performers" cannot see the changing effect of their color movement, they need to be directed from outside, with members taking turns out in front of the group and calling such directions as, "Yellow, move out into the light, with Gray coming in behind, slowly and lower. Now, Dark Gray, in from the other side, up quickly toward center," and so on.

This kind of color study has been used by a class divided into several subgroups and working in a gymnasium, with the color composition framed by a spotlight or between two winglike screens. In practice, almost any group can be expected to develop its own adaptations and departures, taking advantage of special factors in its own situation. Thus one group composed "in the round," to be viewed from all sides and from above. Another worked above a three-foot wall of corrugated cardboard, restricting their moving color to panels of colored cardboard and paper.

Experiment 35:

Color Flip Books

Another effective way to study color sequences, this time by an individual, is to make Flip Books. Using almost any kind of blank book or scratch pad, or a package of large index cards, apply color to the successive pages, either with paint, colored papers, inks, or other color media, so that as the viewer turns or flips the pages he will see a dramatic color development in the color components and their movement. Again, individuals work these out in many different ways. For example, spray enamels have been used as effective coloring agents. Some experimenters design page sequences of color for slower turning rather than for flipping.

An outgrowth of these experiments in color sequence is the use of passing freight train cars as "notation" for an improvised rhythm band. Thus, one "instrument" performs only as long as a blue car is in view, while others are keyed to red, gray, brown, or other colors.

Experiment 36:

Painting a Movie Film

An interesting way to study color sequences within a fixed rate of movement is to paint and project a movie film. Most of us have seen some of the beautifully made films which professionals have painted, one frame at a time, on 35 mm. film; and we probably understand that to achieve such complete control of the medium requires exacting care, great skill and experience. However, with some preparatory planning and instruction, interested amateurs, working on a simple scale, can control the medium enough to compose exciting color action, developing a remarkable variety of color shifts, changes, and combinations.

The directions which follow are for a group, such as a class, working together on this project. By careful preparation of materials and working setup, it has been possible to complete a film sequence in one or, at most, two working sessions. Of course, greater consistency and unity of color relationship can usually be worked out by individuals, and such one-man ventures often follow the introductory experiments in a group.

Preparing Equipment and Supplies

The first requirement is a film projector. Schools usually own the 16 mm. size, but if 8 mm. is the only size available, you can use it. Next, you will need about two hundred feet of old sound or silent film, matched in size to your projector. Almost any film library will be able to provide such an abandoned film. Be sure that its sprocket holes have not been damaged.

To prepare the blank film, work at a sink, or better, a double sink, and wear rubber gloves. Unwind the film into a tub or large pan filled with a strong solution of household chlorine bleach in warm water. The images will soon dissolve. Then pull the film between a folded sponge or coarse cloth to wipe off any remaining streaks of the film coating. Rinse and coil it loosely in a large, open carton to dry. Sometimes space will allow draping the wet film back and forth across inside clothes lines. Be careful to keep the film off the floor where it might be stepped on and damaged. When it is dry and rewound, it is ready for painting.

The easiest way to apply color to film is with colored felt-brush markers (avoid the watercolor type). However, some of these colored inks, when projected, are muddy or weak. You will find brighter, clearer color in "Transparent Removable Acetate Inks," to be applied with brushes. They are obtainable from art supply stores in ¾-ounce bottles. You should get red, yellow, blue, and probably also green, violet, orange, and perhaps brown; but of course you can work with just a few colors. In addition to these transparent colored inks you should also get black "Opaque Removable Acetate Ink." All of these "removable" inks apply easily, dry quickly, can be scraped or scratched, and are soluble in denatured alcohol. You will also find good colors in "Transparent Permanent Acetate Inks," but these require lacquer thinner as a solvent or brush cleaner. If you are preparing for a group, you should plan to have about one bottle of ink per painter. You will need to provide labeled bottles of necessary solvents, within reach of all painters, and rags or paper towels for wiping brushes.

For work with colored inks you will need a supply of small-sized, inexpensive water color brushes, camel's hair or ox hair. You should have at least one brush for each film painter.

Working Setup

Assemble the longest continuous row of tables which your quarters can accommodate and cover them with wrapping paper. Provide good illumination. The film should be unreeled along one edge of the tables, looped around and returned along the other side of the tables, so that a maximum continuous length is ready for painting. The film should be held down every four or five feet by some kind of weight, which may also mark off sections for individual painters. Inks and solvents along the center of the table may be reached by painters from either side.

Understanding the Process

Before painting begins, it is essential for all to know the main technical limitations and possibilities of the medium. First, look at a strip of film which has not been cleaned. If it is 16 mm., count the 16 frames (about 4¾" long) which are projected in one second at silent speed, and the 24 frames (about 7") which go by in one second at sound speed. When you see the very slight change in image from one frame to the next, you will understand why drawn or shaped images would not show unless they were repeated, with gradual shifting for movement. Note how much of the outside edge of the film is not included in the projected image, and see how each separate frame matches up with the sprocket holes.

The main variables are: "Which color? How much (how long or wide)? How dark or light? Similar or contrasting color sequences? One, two, or more colors at once? Long color development or alternation, change, return? Plain color or busy pattern and texture? Shifts in direction of movement?"

Painting Procedures

First, try out your inks, brushes, and markers on a short strip of cleaned film, learning how to avoid puddles of ink, how quickly it dries, how to add other colors on the back. If possible, splice and project these tryout samples, or project other painted film to see effects of similar handling.

73   *Setup for painting 16mm film.*

74   *Sample strips from painted films.*

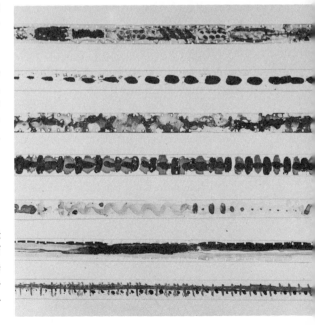

The extent of coordinated planning depends on time and numbers. The most obvious sequences come from each person's color of ink. Thus, if one painter is working with blue and one of his neighbors has green, they can plan to meet suddenly or to shift gradually, in various ways. On later examination, one may decide that blue needs to reappear farther along in the film, and that black should carry through in a texture over the green. Lengthwise strips of color are easiest and usually best, but if used alone they produce a monotonous vertical emphasis when projected. Therefore, crosswise strokes and some frame-by-frame series of spots or strokes, more or less matched to successive sprocket holes, will give useful variety of movement. Unpainted "white" sections are usually least effective. Try scratching the dried ink with knives or scrapers, but avoid cutting film or tearing sprocket holes. The whole film should be painted, with no forgotten gaps. When it is thoroughly dry, rewind it on a reel for projection.

The film is sure to be an exciting visual experience, stimulating some members to apply their discoveries to new ventures. In rerunning the film, the group may try accompanying it with recorded sound—perhaps a percussion record or a "found sound" tape (see Chapter 9).

All of our color experiments have been concerned with color relationships. A good way to analyze your experience is to reexamine one or more of your color experiments and to try to list, not as nouns but as verbs, the kinds of expressive action or behavior you have seen your colors take *as colors*—for example, they echo, dominate, intrude, support, recede. To be helpful, such verbal listing must reflect your own first-hand responses to color. Since words can only approximate color experience, your verbs may not sound "right" to others, but to you they may suggest the significance of that experience. Such noting of color action is especially valuable in looking for color relationships, described earlier.

17

Experiments in Response to Three-Dimensional Space

Special education has drawn upon a wide range of research which shows that learning to read or write requires certain basic sensory/motor skills; and training programs have been designed to help handicapped children differentiate up/down, right/left, near/far, and so on, in relation to their own bodies. In turn, these studies have shed new light on all children's learning processes, including such aesthetic experience as the linear movement we discussed in Chapter 8. We know that movement of this kind requires some consistency, as well as flexibility, in postural orientation to gravity. We also know that groups of muscles must function so that right and left directions are clearly differentiated, whether the "movement" is applied to forming a letter, estimating distance, or working with negative numbers. Training procedures have been carefully developed, ranging from children's floor exercises in right/left discrimination, or laterality, to ingenious programs in eye retaining such as those which have increased the hitting power of major league baseball clubs. Much creative work goes into the designing of these useful exercises. But an important problem in special education, and indeed in all education, is how to combine such training in skills with processes of self-realization and expressive statement.

The process of identifying oneself with any three-dimensional space includes linear movement, real or imagined, within that space, and stems from a more or less clear body image as the point of perceptual origin or reference.

Space is perceived through clues which must be interpreted and developed as concepts, rather than perceived directly as are colors. These clues are mainly visual and auditory, but the most direct of them involve movement itself, or the estimated movement which we feel as the muscle tensing of kinesthesis. Visual clues described by students of perception include: various kinds of perspective; the comparative size of images; overlap; the changing tensions of the lens accomodation in the eye and in the divergent movement of the two eyes focusing; the matching of the two views seen (stereopsis); and the difference in apparent movement of near and far

75   *Space invention.*

76   *Semi-privacy.*

objects (movement parralax). To these clues are added the radar types of sound waves which help us perceive space. Much research is being devoted to the processes by which we deal with all of these patterns of clues and is shedding light on both the fumbling beginnings and the most refined extensions of responding to space.

In order that we respond in terms of aesthetic/creative experience, the world of space which we perceive should be sufficiently dependable so that we can risk reaching out to reorganize it. We must have at least begun to control it so that we can assert, "I see and I say," with some feeling of personal joy and confidence.

The ability to deal with perceptual clues in order to structure space is important to us because it allows us to comprehend and to work with *relationships*: of things in our physical environment, such as approaching cars, and of conceptualization, such as the grouping of mathematics, the extent of time, or the envisioned image or construction. Some assurance, earned and tested, of orientation in space is prerequisite to work with alternative possibilities in problem solving and, on a much wider scale, in preparatory phases of creative work. You must be able to say, "Here I am," before you can ask, "How would it be if . . . ?"

Considering the fundamental importance of spatial awareness to thinking/feeling processes, it is remarkable how we leave to chance its development. When included in our teaching plans, it is usually prescribed as training exercises with walking beams, chalkboard templates, climbing ladders, moving lights, and other mechanical procedures. Whereas working with color is considered to encompass much beyond the reading of traffic signals, working with space is generally thought of in terms of some minimal adequacy. This is probably because of failure to recognize the possibilities of highly developed, personal expression through the construction, ordering, and modifying of space. We know the individuality of handwriting, and we can learn to see personal uniqueness in the movement of the performing artist and in the form of the clay and "assemblages" of the individual sculptor. But the possibility of a developed, even great, personal space statement is usually beyond our experience, even though much of what we know of individual children, for example, comes through noting differences in such expressive spatial factors as the style and scale of their two- and three-dimensional arranging, and their way of using floor or playground space and "spacing out" their actions in time.

In most environmental situations we overlook spatial relationships because we are busy responding to things. Sometimes these things define or characterize the space, but their identity as isolated objects, made to stand out, perhaps, by their color, shape, brightness, or movement, takes precedence over their relationships; and what we experience in viewing them is a list of separate visual events related chiefly by "and."

The experiments which follow are designed to increase our awareness of how we work with space and how space works with us, especially in the volumes of our three-dimensional environment.

77   *Spatial selection . . .*

Responding to Spatial Differences

Experiment 37:

Observing Immediate Space Setting

Some sites have been specifically prepared as spatial vantage points, such as observation towers on skyscrapers or lookout stops beside mountain roads. But most of the space relationships of our environments are not so labeled and may go unnoticed. For example, the reader may stop to look at the immediate, three-dimensional space within which he now finds himself. To do so he must go beyond listing this as page, that as thumb, table top, knee, or chair leg, and must move his eyes so as to construct the space, as it extends from face plane to book-hand mass, along table-arm-lap, into overhung cage below chair, and so on.

focus on planes . . . into space setting.

The perception of space depends primarily on our body movement, actual or imagined, but our aesthetic response is less affected by such factors as objective dimension (the number of paces across a narrow street, for example) than by the way the space relates to us, as when the buildings "press in on us" so that we go along the street between the walls with our movement and feeling of movement shaped by the space. Much of this feeling depends, of course, on what space we came from, how long we continue to move in the narrowness, how it varies, and into what it leads, or is expected to lead.

A good way to experience such movement in space is to explore one's immediate environment in search of a series of spatial changes through which to walk.

78 from . . .

down . . .

Experiment 38:

Finding and Taking a Space Walk

Starting from where you are, think of the usual, as well as unusual, paths you might take to move through nearby, clearly characterized spaces (staying, of course, within limits of safety, if not of comfort). Then go and try them out. You may find many of these move-through paths within your building, or under or over it, or between it and its neighbors. Indeed, such a listing of positional relationships of yourself to the space will guide your search and describe your findings: into, out of, toward, away from, along, through, up, down, under, over, against, across, around, between, and so on. For example, seeing an open doorway, you go through it into a dark passage between one unbroken wall surface and another consisting of doors. You turn to a larger door, opening onto a hallway. Here, stairs go up and down out of sight. You descend as usual, except that now you look through the railing as it passes, observe the surface sloping just above your head, and question

on down . . .   *into . . .*

alternative passages leading away from landings. Perhaps you go down an extra level into the unfamiliar coolness of a basement corridor. Walking below pipes, you may pass a grating with dim shapes of storage behind it, cross a wide, low room divided by columns, and descend more steps into the furnace room. Later you may come up into an areaway to peer up through attics, under balconies, over bridges, and up ramps, ducking under or squeezing past obstacles, fumbling through drapes, peering through screens, climbing down ladders, and so on, depending on what is available and how far you wish to venture.

In such exploring of space, you will be asking several kinds of questions. One would be how the space affects your moving in the directional relationships, such as along, around, through or down, cited earlier. For example, did it channel, invite, block, break, continue, or focus your movement? A second question would be its main effect on your feeling—what happened to you, what were your changing impressions, such as hiding,

through . . .   *out . . .*

standing exposed, being compressed, hurried, confused, freed, or threatened? A third would ask the chief affecting factor in the various space situations experienced. Some of these factors will doubtless refer to the floor or base on which you were walking—its degrees of regularity, changes in levels, or variations in textures. Another affecting factor might be found overhead, or in the degrees of permeability (either "see-through" or "go-through" possibilities) in surrounding surfaces. What seemed to suggest spatial continuation, and what indicated a deadend? Were there intevening objects, dividers, or obstructions? Was movement spatially predicted, or were open alternatives and surprises offered?

In addition to factors of three-dimensional form, are there others such as degrees of light, color relationship, sound, temperature, smells, or dampness which affect your space experience?

over . . .   *up . . .*

All of these questions, applied to each of the space experiences you have found, help you ask, "How is it?" and "Why is it that way?" Probably the most important question remains, "How does one space experience lead out of and on into others?"

Design a Space Walk

The next part of this experiment is to select and arrange a space walk which, in its emphases, shifts, and continuations, offers an organized space experience which is coherent, interesting, and significant for the participant. Your sensing of space differences will guide your hunches and choices. There will be occasions when the space factors are clear, strong, and inviting, and others when they are complex and even confusing. There will be sensations of constriction or tension and others of expansion or relaxation. Continuing, almost monotonous

and up . . .

on up . . .

spaces may offer a variety of small but intriguing differences, then they may lead into sudden, dramatic contrasts, as in scale, proportion, or timing. Such contrasts need not involve real danger, violence, or commando-course feats to evoke a full range of response to space. To find a sequence of clearly characterized spatial situations, you will need to avoid all kinds of distracting elements which might clutter and weaken the experience.

Sharing Your Experience

After you have tried out your space walk design and perhaps modified or reorganized it, you will be ready to call on friends and associates who might be open to such possibilities and invite them to participate in your space walk adventure.

Some instructions such as the following may add to their experience: "I've been looking at the space setups we move around in. I was trying to look not at the *things*

on top . . .

and around . . .

we are surrounded with, but at the spaces between them, and not just floor space, but up and down, along corridors, overhead, through doors, seeing through things, and so on. I'd like to take you on a little walk so you can see for yourself. I'll go ahead to show you the way and I'll stay in sight; but we won't be talking during the walk. When we get back, though, we'll talk over how it was."

The discussion after the walk might begin with the simple questions, "How was it?" Inexperience in reporting such relationships as those of a space sequence, and lack of vocabulary for expressing such responses may lead the participants simply to list the things they have seen, but your "how" questions may help them to bring out qualitative differences in their experiences. As the "designer," you will be interested in the way they may share or differ with your own ideas and feelings about the space walk.

down into . . .

between . . .

from below . . .

on to . . .

across . . .

down from above.

79   *Notation of a space walk.*

Other Space Trips

Experiment 39:

City Space Walk

A sequence of space experiences such as we have been examining could be found in most houses, apartment buildings, schools, or in a group of buildings in a city block. On a different scale, the architectonic qualities of these space settings may also be found in travelling about a city, with its changes in levels, width of passage, height of ceiling, and long views, surprise turns, dead ends, and cubbyholes.

A city's arrangements for traffic and transportation often provide a remarkable variety of space experience. Tunnels, roadways, balconies, escalators, elevators, parking lots, and waiting rooms offer much more than the shortest line from here to there. One's response to their space variations is, of course, affected by changes in concentrations of people, as between the asparaguslike bunching in a rush hour elevator and the long, tense approach of the single passer-by in an early morning walk through a tunnel.

Planning a city trip which is interesting because it provides clearly felt variations in spatial experience is an informative extension of the smaller-scaled space walk experiment. Using yourself as the moving point of (perceptual) origin, you can take your psychological radar into the city's canyons, shafts, slopes, runways, plazas, hideaways, and promontories. And again, you can share and check your city space design with a friend—"from trap-like pocket to lofty crow's nest in twenty minutes," or whatever your discoveries offer.

Experiment 40:

Approaching Home

Most young people of today have never observed the long-gaited enthusiasm of a horse "heading for the barn." But they have experienced, or at least vaguely felt, the quickening crescendo of the return to home at day's end. What goes into that? How, indeed, do we know we are getting to the district, the street, the block, the building, the door? By reading signs? By counting steps or corners? Assign yourself this basic, personal space question, and over several days study all the clues and signals you may have been taking for granted.

Experiment 41:

Comparing Parks

City space is experienced not only by moving through it but also by stopping to look around and to "be" in it. For example, go to a park and observe it actively as a spatial organization; that is, move into it from different sides, wander along its paths, sit on its benches, and look around and up through its trees. In short, experience what it has to offer you as a space setting. Then give the same participating kind of study to another park and compare, first, your considered response to the over-all spatial character of each and, secondly, the effective space factors which make the difference.

The kind of study of town and city which we have been suggesting can be extended and focused to produce a new appreciation of differences in our civic living space. One of our most urgent needs is to develop an informed, responsible, citizen participation in the visual character of city centers and neighborhoods; unfortunately, this is a need which our schools seem least prepared to meet. For example, many Americans are beginning to question the endless rows of identical living boxes with which we have celebrated our skill in mass production. A contrasting anarchy may disturb them vaguely as they drive along grubby miles of roadside businesses, each waving its clamoring sign to outshout all the others. Deliberations and decisions of city planners, zoning boards, highway commissions, and authorities responsible for our parks, beaches, rivers, and forests all need the trained eyes and discriminating judgment of a jealous citizenry. New generations of young people, able to bring some aesthetic response to moving through our common space, could become a positive force for a humane environment.

American mobility is everywhere apparent, in the first grade's walking to the post office or the social studies class on its trip to the capitol, in the family towing its trailer household, and in thousands pouring out of a subway. We need to bring to such increasing movement a rich background of specific, personal response to spatial differences. Being told or observing how space is organized and how "it" feels must be backed by a wide range of convincing personal experiences in space making and space modifying. The experiments in the next chapter suggest approaches to such study. As usual, the place to start work is close to home, in the architecture of where we live, but without feeling that "our" space is restricted inside any door.

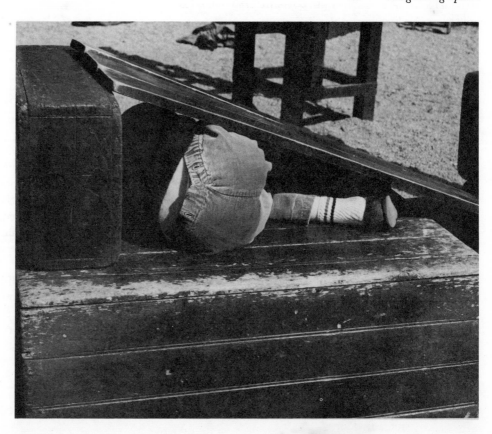

18

Experiments in Constructing and Modifying Three-Dimensional Space

Formerly, interior design began with a drawing of each wall of a room and perhaps others of its floor and ceiling, on the theory that (1) we live in boxes, and (2) designing living space means designing the sides of the boxes. Sometimes these sides had holes in them for walking or seeing through, but enough flat wall and floor were left to hold the things that belonged in the box.

Another way of laying out a living space is shown by animals who, far from field or forest, turn around and around before they lie down. Here "form follows function" not only by fitting the body's dimensions but also by providing a comforting security within which to go to sleep. In order to study living space, one must look into processes of living rather than conventions of building.

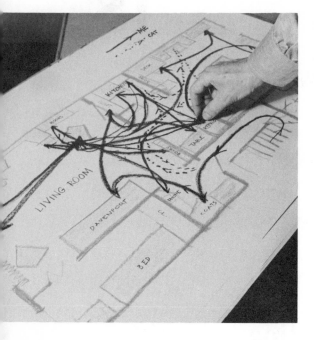

81   *Trails weave a shape in living space.*

Experiment 42:

Recording Use of Living Area

In order to sample how your own living fits your living space, make a rough drawing of the floor plan of your room, apartment, or home. Without bothering about exact measurements or ruled lines, try to describe the proportions and relationships accurately. Locate doors, windows, and closets, and sketch in the floor space occupied by the main pieces of furniture. Then, using a different kind of pen, pencil, or crayon, draw in the trail of all your movement in a specified period, perhaps the first half hour after you get home from work or after you get up in the morning, adding arrow heads to show the direction of each movement. (Figure 81 shows an example.) You could add different auxiliary trails, as of a pet or of another person, if this would help to show the "shape of living" in that space. Your recorded lines of movement will probably take on a main shape, with minor offshoots, and will no doubt appear mainly in certain sections of the available floor space, leaving other parts almost untouched.

Other times and functions might show different use of the space, and a record of that use would need to show kinds of activities other than locomotion, for example, the sight lines of individuals watching television or slide projection, or of a mother watching a baby, and the conversation lines within groups and subgroups.

The importance of shaping and reshaping the environment to enable certain kinds of living is well known to the teacher of young children, who learns to include a kind of predictive stage management in her work with individuals and groups. In families, too, the spatial form of living may vary greatly at different times and occasions, even within cramped quarters.

We are accustomed to thinking of these living shapes only as floor pattern, or at least as taking place on a flat floor; but many exciting bull sessions have developed in dormitories, for example, with participants not only in chairs and standing, but also lounging in upper and lower bunks, and seated on desk, table, and floor. Such heights and levels often seem to help the speaking, listening, and thinking on such occasions. The varied terrain around a camp fire may offer similar advantages, leading to such domesticated adaptations as living room balconies, sunken hearths, and conversation pits. Hopefully, however, most living spaces will become the setting for some unpredictable events, which might call for flexibility in spatial modification.

82   *Levels affecting interchange.*

Experiment 43:

Levels Affecting Interaction

Be on the lookout for instances of communication when
you and your companions are on different levels, not
only within a room but also in such settings as window
to street, up and down stairs, on a balcony, in a cellar,
inside and outside a car, and so on. See how your own
location in such three-dimensional relationships affects
the interchange.

Stage designers know how levels of steps, ramps, balconies and bridges, as well
as other kinds of spatial separation and connection, fit and enhance the communication of feeling. The variation in the actor's positional relationships are "read" by
the audience as part of the expression of speech and movement.

Experiment 44:

Observing Architectonic Space Elements

A variety of environmental space studies can be made with simple planes of cardboard.

Experiment 44A:

Moving Across a Plane

If you hold a piece of cardboard horizontally and just below eye level, you can "traverse" the plazalike plane, either as eye movement or, with practice, as imagined movement of your (inch-high) self. The latter kind of bodily projection and identification may begin falteringly, but it results in much better space participation. Having crossed the plane, you come to the edge or boundary, to be walked along or peered over. Since this "reading yourself in" departs from our usual ways of observing, give plenty of time to it.

Experiment 44B:

Walls Stop or Deflect

Stood vertically before you on a table's surface, the plane will become a flat, uncompromising wall or barrier, but turned away slightly, it may suggest moving away along its base.

Experiment 44C:

Into a Corner

With a second vertical cardboard, you can stop the movement along the wall by setting up a corner; this can be changed to either a deep pocket or shallow bay.

Experiment 44D:

Opening Out

If the two planes of your corner are held apart, very different possibilities appear, inviting movement through the opening. But changing the relationship of the two

83 *Seeing your way into a sharp corner.*

planes can vary the invitation of the opening, from a simple gap in a flat wall to a funnellike exit to be squeezed through, to a transition into a partly hidden continuation of the visible space.

Experiment 44E:

Continuing Space

Visual continuity is produced by the unbroken wall plane which, along with the floor plane, connects the seen space with the partly seen space beyond the open corner—an important principle in contemporary architecture. Try lighting one section more than the other and note the effect.

Experiment 44F:

Overhead

Join the two sloping planes above your eye level and look up into a steeply pitched and shadowed roof. Again, vary the slopes and let in an overhead strip of clerestory light.

Experiment 44G:

Canyon

On the table, stand the planes parallel and close together, and peer into the long, narrow, lofty corridor. Spread the walls at the far end for a gradual opening up.

Experiment 44H:

Room

Hold the planes parallel again, but this time horizontal, and look into a wide, low-ceilinged room. Change the ceiling height and observe its effect on your "movement."

You will find many other ways in which your planes can change the feeling of movement in space.

Experiment 45:

Inter-plane Space Constructions

Next try intersecting the two cardboard planes at some point by cutting a slit into the edge of each. Each slit should be cut twice so it is just wide enough to receive the thickness of the other cardboard. Of course, you can vary the length, location, and direction of the slits as you wish. Now try standing the joined, intersecting planes on the table in all possible positions, studying all the movements possible in their partially enclosed spaces. You will probably find that one of the positions in which you stand the planes will provide for a more interesting variety of movement.

84   *Slits allow planes to intersect.*

85   *Planes define space . . .*

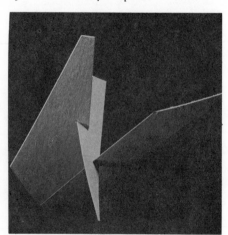

86   *. . . to move into . . .*

Now you are ready to work with several cardboard planes of different size and shape, to work out a space structure which, when viewed from any direction, will invite interesting and varied spatial movements. You should have access to a variety of simple shapes—oblongs, strips and elongated triangles—perhaps in different weights of cardboard and cut on a paper cutter. Two additional techniques, besides slitted intersections, may facilitate construction: scoring the cardboard with mat knife or scissors point and ruler if you wish to fold a plane, and setting your construction on a base, perhaps of corrugated board cut from a carton. Such a base will allow you to tack down cardboard corners or edges with straight pins until you are ready to fasten them with drops of glue. Since space study, not product making, is our purpose, permanence is unimportant.

87   *and under . . .*   88   *. . . in many variations.*

You will need to turn the work and study it from every angle, especially at eye level (see Figure 88). Again, try to imagine that it is a great, soaring structure, perhaps fifty or a hundred feet high, and that you are walking around it, through it, under its overhangs, up its ramps, and out onto its balconies and roofs. If pockets and dead ends appear, study them, for they may be helpful variations; but if a wall tends to divide the structure and to block long movements, it may need to be raised or broken into. You may wish to introduce some curved planes, or even a few connecting/dividing/guiding lines of thread or rods, but try to avoid the temptation to make just a pretty object. Instead, focus on the movement invited by the spatial volumes and how you feel to "be" in it.

Your space study will probably be facilitated by avoiding the complex effects of different colors in your structural planes. The contrast between black and yellow walls, for example, might drown out any subtle shadows of shape. But do try experimenting with colored planes, to see how they behave.

89   *Built to invite movement.*

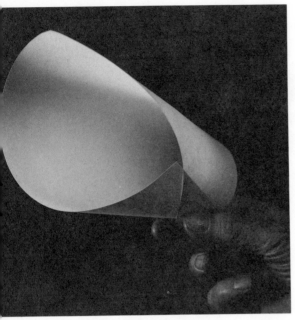

Of course, cardboard plane structures need not be standing "buildings" on bases; they can be suspended from above or hung on a wall so as to be looked into and studied from many angles.

Experiment 46:

Curved Plane Space Structures

Working with an easily curved sheet of white bond or mimeograph paper is advantageous for space study. First, observe the austere beauty of the curving plane, its subtly changing shadows, sweeping edges, and inside/outside contrast (see Figure 91). Then cut into the sheet one or more times, and without removing or adding parts, curve out subordinate volumes with different axes and added possibilities for spatial movement. Study the construction from every side, avoiding impenetrable views and confused "traffic jams." If the form becomes too complicated, start over. Fasten the construction with a minimum of pins, staples or tongues in slits, and hang it up to see the variety of its spatial organization.

90   *Inside-outside beauty.*

91   *Soaring space structure.*

Experiment 47:

Irregular Plane Space Structure

Constructing space with flat or curved planes can produce a geometrical clarity in the inscribed movement.

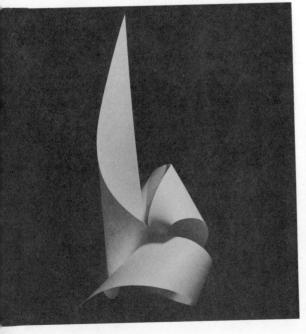

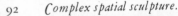

92   *Complex spatial sculpture.*

In order to observe a less simple space structure, take a large sheet of paper, perhaps newsprint, and gather and crumple it slowly into a wad, without any formal folding or curving. Then release it and help it to open gradually until its rumpled structure begins to show narrow pockets, jagged rooms and large, angular passages. As it is opened up, try turning it on different sides until you find the approach which invites the most varied space participation. Construct and study several variations of these accidental space structures in different kinds of paper, and then try an informally draped cloth, such as a rumpled cotton sheet dropped over a chair or piled casually on a table.

Experiment 48:

Shell Structure for Imaginary Playground

A more manageable and flexible medium for space experiments is clay, rolled out in slabs or sheets one-quarter to three-eighths inch thick. Pound out the clay on a piece of damp muslin, using a rolling pin or wooden scraper to bring it to an even thickness and surface. Cut simple shapes and stand them in place on a clay slab base, arching and joining the planes, doming them out, and cutting openings to provide the greatest variety of possible settings for climbing, hiding, sliding, as equipment for children's play (see Figure 95). Study the structure from all sides to see how the inside and outside spaces are articulated. Using a light may help.

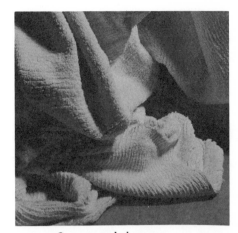

93   *Caverns and chasms.*
94   *Rolling out a clay slab.*

95   *Making a shell setting for space play . . .   or a more rugged structure . . .   or more complex.*

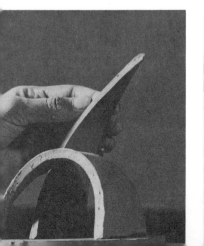

Experiment 49:

The Space Box

An intriguing way to study the effects of space modification is to begin with a sturdy, empty box of any size
from a candy or shoe box to a small carton. At first simply look inside until you begin to "feel at home" in its
volume and dimensions. The problem is to make "being" and "moving" in there more interesting or more
significant as a space experience; in other words, to develop that volume as the space setting for the viewer's
best possible visual participation in its three-dimensional organization. You may use any means to effect
any changes you wish in the shape, with one execption:
no occupying feature, object, or "actor" is to be put
into the setting, since the viewer (yourself) is to be the
inhabiting participant. The space box, an interesting
vacant room, is not to be confused with the diorama.

Many kinds of materials may be drawn upon in this
experiment, although the variety combined in any one
space box should be limited by careful selection. Various
kinds of planes will be needed: for example, some with
the opaque rigidity of cardboard, others which are patterned, colored, translucent, transparent, or textured, as
in papers or fabrics. The free lines of threads, yarns, and
tapes, the controlled lines of wires, the stiff lines of rods,
sticks, or reeds, and the many kinds of textured stuffs all
may be useful. The technical problems of fitting, cutting, and fastening could, of course, tax a skilled crafts-
man, but most of these can be cut short or bypassed if
permanence and portability are not important. Pinning
parts in place while a drop of white plastic glue dries
will solve most of the fastening problems.

More important than fitting and fashioning are choosing and arranging. Here are some questions to help you
begin the work:

Do you like the proportions of the space? Would your
first reaction to it, as a lofty lightness or a low dungeon,
for example, be better served if the box were turned,
cut down, or extended?

Do you like looking through an open side or should the opening be reduced? To a peep hole?

Is it too dark in there? Where would you like to let in a beam of light?

Do you like the flat expanse of the floor, the walls, and the ceiling? Would you prefer a sloping, curving, or crumpled surface? A different color?

Would a break in the space, like a column of stretched string or a poked-through rod (or several of them) help to lead your eye in? Would a partial screen, as of netting or other see-through material, provide a degree of separation? Should these intervals be constructed on a slant or a right angle?

96   *Cut a window for a light beam.*

Holes in cover for lighting and viewing.

Move through, toward the light.   Optical tricks.

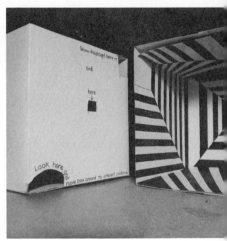

What would aid "moving about" in the space—ramps, directional guide lines, balconies, partitions, platforms?

How would it feel to "be" in there. Is it too harsh and clean cut? Would some textural softening or reduced light help? Is it too abrupt, too brief? Would mirrors extend it? Would color transparencies help?

97   *Jewelled cave of egg separators.*

As you work, the space will begin to acquire a special character, as of cold, mist, gloom, turbulence, delicacy, or sweep. You will find yourself working along with that character, using it as your direction and touchstone. But treat this character as space, to express "how it would be to be in there." And work with factors of setting rather than additional symbolic objects.

Finally, you might try to give your space box a title which would suggest the direction of its character or special space quality.

Building Space Awareness with Blocks

One of the most rewarding (and underestimated) ways to study architectonic space is to work with unit building blocks. For many years they have ranked first in the equipment of the nursery school and kindergarten, but until recently, their usefulness for adults' study has been generally overlooked, except by some of our great architects.

From watching children work with blocks, we understand some of their values. Grasping the clearly defined shapes and lifting, moving, and placing them are muscular work; but close observation shows how the hands of even a three-year-old, in placing one block on top of another, come to include a swift but sure and sensitive check for its stability before they move on to another block. We see the child's assurance of his own standing up as he makes the block stand up; and when he adds to the to-and-fro of track building, the inside-outside of enclosures, the under-over of bridges and shelters, and the up-down-through-behind of towers, he is achieving secure orientation of his body in three-dimensional space.

98   *Building sure orientation in space.*

Although blocks are pleasant to hold and to move about, their substance, color, and texture remain the same. The sure way they fit together, with their multiple dimensions and regular shapes, is also a constant, even though growing experience makes estimates of their fit, in structure or on storage shelf, more and more accurate and sure. They are indeed modular materials with which one "makes" only by organizing them in positional relationships. In this arranging, the thrust and reach of the block forms are perceived to a large extent kinesthetically, as a muscular statement in space.

Blocks are rightfully valued in teaching quantitative relationships, and certainly they instill not only the fact but also the feeling of length times width times thickness or the even fit of what is "equal." But an arithmetic achievement test will not reflect the main contribution of block building.

Blocks are also valuable as instruments of dramatic play with toy trucks, trains, boats, and dolls. Although imagining oneself as a participant in the spatial organization of blocks is an important part of an aesthetic response to them, the stories one makes up, like "all aboard for Staten Island," are poor measures of the essential value of block building.

The reader is urged to find a set of building blocks and to work with them because they offer, in helpfully simplified form, a direct approach to space construction, emphasizing the rich variables of orientation, scale, mass, and interval pattern.

99   *Spatial variations with three blocks.*

Experiment 50:

Space Construction with Blocks

If possible, you should gain access to a good sized set of standard unit building blocks. You will need mostly the straight blocks, and also the ramps, triangles, cylinders and "roof boards." Less important, and probably distracting, are the elaborate gothic doors, elliptical curves, arches, and switches.

Working on a large, uncluttered floor, as in a gymnasium, is ideal, provided you are prepared, physically and in dress, to get down and peer into your constructions. As an alternative, you may work on the surface of joined tables, as large and extensive as possible, but placed so you can work from all sides and reach into the center.

To begin with, you need only about a dozen simple blocks, such as squares, units, double units, and boards. Set one of them before you and look at it, all around it. Stand it another way, and another, studying the changes. Put a second block next to and in line with it, then offset behind or in front of it, or somewhat separated from it, walking around to observe the resulting continuities, breaks, and intervals. Lay a board on top of them, shifting it to line up with certain surfaces and to provide a sheltering overhang. Try many arrangements of these three blocks, observing the full three-dimensional effect in each case. Thoroughness and patience in these early stages will focus your attention on the main question: the space experience inscribed or defined by the relationship of the block forms.

As you extend your space structure with other blocks, selecting and placing will be guided by their effect on possibilities of living inside, outside, over, under, through, along, behind, toward, away from, against, or in line with the space. Study the structure from every side and especially from floor level. A movable light like a desk lamp is a great help in observing the in-and-out relationships and may lead to ideas for some photography later on.

100 *Construction guided by possibilities of movement*

Avoid the common mistake of simply adding on or piling up blocks. For example, boxlike structures, no matter how big and solid, usually suggest very limited spatial movement. And if a tower at one end of a long, courtlike extension looms up effectively, simply adding others may cancel that effect. Falling into automatic or mechanical kinds of sing-song logic usually reflects a failure to move around and within the structure. Past conditioning often leads us into formally symmetrical arrangements, with the stately immobility and self-centeredness of wedding cakes or grave stones. Formal structures should be restudied to discover their relationship with more distant factors of neighborhood or other new settings.

Work with the orientation of your structures as they lead out into and connect up with larger spaces or other structures. Perhaps a low wall or a row of small forms can mark out or suggest a direction and lead the eye toward or away from your structure into a larger space organization. In turn, your awareness of such extending relationships may affect the outlook quality of your central structure itself.

101   *Study your construction from near the floor level . . .*

Try departing from the usual methods of piling up blocks and bridging from post to post. Instead, cantilever long, projecting overhangs by using counterweights. Along with such mechanical ventures, try visual counterbalancing, such as an echoing vertical or projecting niche reappearing toward the end of a wall or promontory.

Anticipation of a final tumbling crash is probably an overrated feature of block building compared with the

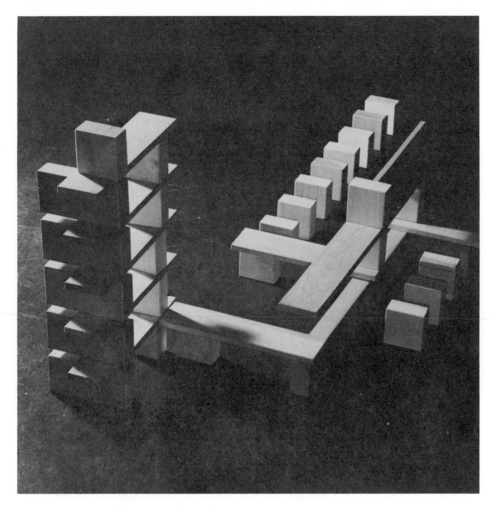

102   *. . . and look in from every angle.*

departures and surprises possible within the space of a
block structure, and even more so in a large gymnasium
community of many informally related block structures.
While you may find some of the grand sweep and long
axes of Pennsylvania Avenue, the Place de la Concorde,
or the approach to the Taj Mahal, you will more likely
find the kind of informal variety, shifts, and contrasts in
space organization which give meaning to parades and
vistas. It is in the intervals and passages of their spacing,
rather than in the mechanics of their piling, that blocks
provide important aesthetic experience.

Encouraging Creativity: The Teacher's Role

Behind the many experiments we have asked you to try were two purposes: first, to help you discover in yourself new possibilities for constructive enjoyment, and second, to help you gain insights into *what helps* this kind of discovery and invention. While we have worked with many materials and productive processes, we have always kept an eye on aesthetic and creative *experience*. Moreover, we have seen that such experience takes place essentially within an independent, individual organism and that outside help, while it may contribute greatly to the experience, is only an environmental condition affecting individual behavior.

We know that it is the teacher who is, or can be, the most effective factor in this outside help. Of course, there are some teachers who "simplify" the creative process by reducing it to steps of prescribed production, and there are others, often honestly baffled, who withdraw from the children's working situation and take almost no part beyond overall management of supplies and physical setting. Either of these well-meant approaches can contribute to the burial of creative potential.

There are, however, positive ways in which the teacher can encourage children's aesthetic and creative development. We shall discuss four of them, to see both how they have affected our own ventures and how they may help our teaching.*

1. Permitting

The teacher can permit, allow for, or provide opportunity for aesthetic/creative experience by:

Offering many varied occasions for children's sensory play, experiment, and growth at their own pace.

Accepting and welcoming their responses, feelings, interests, and plans.

Valuing children's variations and off-beat departures rather than insisting on conformity to norms or predetermined goals.

Keeping the program flexible for learning.

The child needs psychological "elbow room" if he is to assert himself in free, independent action rather than move only as a result of pressures outside himself. To be useful to the child, such psychological room must have some definition and known boundaries, for who would venture to leap into the air if he could not assume that some kind of ground would be down there to land upon?

What constitutes "enough room" for aesthetic/creative growth will vary with each child, from the one who finds freedom for his sensing and imagining within the formality of a fire drill to another who, in a phase of rebellion, may be looking only for reasons why he cannot move, no matter what the setting. A child's feeling of freedom for movement is built up gradually out of a long series of small ventures and tests. The teacher, who wants each child to have the highest possible quality of experiencing, will be alert to signs from him that he has enough freedom and is at work on his own.

Sometimes teachers themselves, bowed down by outside pressures and limitations, become paralyzed and unable to take positive action with existing possibilities. Their narrowing expectations will reduce open planning and tolerance of variation unless they too can begin to feel some freedom of movement in teaching and learning.

---

*This section is adapted from the author's "Sensing and Responding to the World: Aesthetic Development" in *Curriculum for Today's Boys and Girls,* Robert S. Fleming, ed. (Columbus, Ohio: Charles E. Merrill Books, Inc., 1963).

In classroom practice the two most critical factors in permitting aesthetic/ creative experience are *time* and *choice*.

Although time for art is sometimes, "Color while the others are finishing their reading," or perhaps, "She doesn't come till Thursday," most schools schedule regular periods for work with a variety of art materials; these periods can be important permitting factors for children's learning. But there also need to be possibilities for building learning-with-feeling out of all of the children's lively interests, whenever they occur. A teacher who has learned to value aesthetic/creative experience will always want more than humdrum learning for his children, in an art period or in any other period.

104   *Notice: Child at work.*

Whenever individual involvement develops, the rigidity of schedules can become a threat. The teacher must insist on some degree of time flexibility, not for its own sake, but because he values important learning experiences for children. This does not mean always drifting from one activity into another "whenever you are ready," for sometimes children welcome the challenge of deadlines; but it does mean that, far from being a baby sitter by the hour or a waiter serving subject courses, the teacher knows he is fostering the qualitative growth which a package-loving, button-pushing society sorely needs.

How many *choices* of activities or media and how many ways to use them do children need for aesthetic/creative growth? Although concentrated digging is the goal, it must be voluntary. This means that the child must find his own ground to dig in, and he needs a wide choice of activities in order to find it. From his own experience the teacher is aware of possible pressures, such as past praise, dependence on another, or fear of the unknown, which may affect the child's choices. The freeing effect of aprons or of having enough materials often enables such a child to risk the possibility of failure in working out his own idea. Because children differ so much in their response to choices, the teacher may need to step in and give them positive reassurance, to help remove barriers and foster real freedom of choice.

2. Inviting

The teacher can *invite,* encourage, or stimulate children's aesthetic/creative experience by:

Planning with the children, both in open discussion and in sensing their interests and readiness.

Offering possibilities for first-hand, vivid, personal perceptions, as with trips, resources brought into classrooms, new materials and equipment.

Asking questions to encourage personal, felt responses.

Having one's interest and energy *invited* is not the same as being cajoled or persuaded to move toward a goal predetermined by someone else. For example, holding up a model of a finished product may stimulate the children's wish to make one like it; or demonstrating how it is produced may invite their interest in seeing if they can do it, too. Although these approaches are direct and fast ways to get a group of children to work, by themselves they do not invite the individual child to raise his own questions or to draw upon his own experience and interests.

In the classroom, most motivating invitations are necessarily offered in the whole-group situation; but the teacher knows that effective aesthetic/creative response is individual, freely given, and usually more like departure from rather than acceptance of the general invitation. Thus, attractive and workable materials—"that

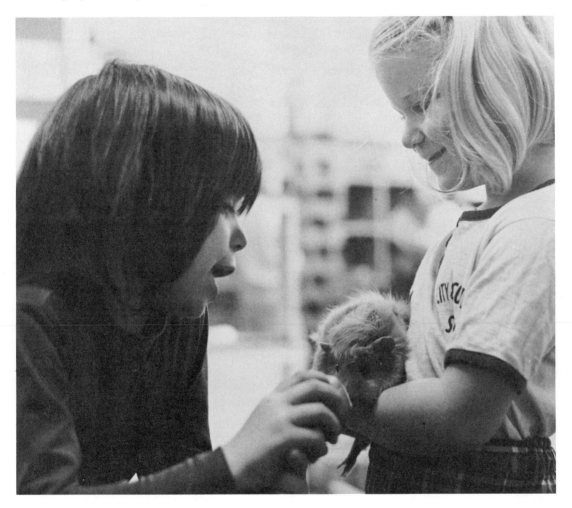

105   *Inviting vivid, personal response.*

yummy stuff"—will interest most children, but moving on to such personal planning as, "What if I . . . ?" may require reassurance.

For example, a third grade group was working in clay. One boy wanted help in modelling Snoopy, his pet rabbit. The teacher asked, "What is he like?" When the boy hesitated, she said, "Show me with your hands." He cupped his hands together and said, "He sits there like a ball, round and soft," and added, "When he's watching me, his ears stand up straight, like this." As she left him the teacher said, "Just work with the clay and make your own Snoopy. He'll turn out fine, you just wait and see."

This teacher sensed that the child was interested but needed to connect the image in his mind's eye with the clay in his hands.

3. Focusing

The teacher can help children *focus* on, become more involved in, or delve more deeply into aesthetic/creative experiences by:

Asking questions to help the child reach the core of the present aesthetic experience, no matter what the form of his work. The teacher observes the child and asks himself, "With what question is the child working?" Thus in clay or blocks the "pay-off" question would probably be related to three-dimensional form, in paints it would be color, and so on.

Helping children to set up a priority in materials they will include and work with the materials they will exclude. Which should the teacher bring out, which should be kept in reserve, available but out of sight?

Encouraging a hunt for similar aesthetic qualities in the environment, such as gradual *vs.* sudden changes in light/dark.

Making reference to related arts to deepen or reinforce experience, for example, sound in visual pattern, or body movement identified with plastic or structural form.

Helping children see qualities in works of art which are similar to what they are working with.

Timing children's sharing of their work to deepen rather than diffuse the experience.

Elsewhere in this book we have discussed the use of found materials in school art activities.* If children's finding of these materials is to lead to aesthetic/creative learning, the teacher will need to help the children focus on inventive and expressive possibilities in materials, rather than merely to name and classify them.

An important question here is whether such a wealth of materials will lead to distraction and confusion of the children's learning experience. Can they focus their attention and work intensively in the presense of many alternatives? How much is too much, how much is enough, and why? Many of the experiments we have asked you to try were designed to raise just these questions.

Occasionally we see a young child, made weary and goggle-eyed by a plethora of exciting new presents, retire to his bed with a well-worn, stuffed animal. He is reminding us that it takes time to make something one's own. Similarly, older children need time to make found objects their own materials. Gradual building of one's own resources is quite different from the sudden acquisition of "one of everything."

Selection, not accumulation, leads to quality in an aesthetic act. Working in collage, for example, may become diffuse and distracting; but it can also facilitate

---

*See Appendix, p. 177.

such choices as, "Is it better with it or without it? Here, down there? More? Next to that?" and so on. As a child shows increasing interest in such visual design questions, his teacher can show him ways to make quick try-out tests so that such choosing may be clear, confident, and not dependent on formulas.

Helping children to see *more* in *less* becomes increasingly important as they grow up exposed to a commercial downpour of sensational stimuli. The danger is not that they will come to prefer strong colors to subtle colors or driving rhythms to more complex musical structure, but rather that they will become unresponsive, unresourceful, bored, with "nothing to do."

Anyone's ventures into aesthetic construction grow from or draw upon past experience, on the one hand, and open up or lead into new experience on the other; this growth may be expressed as "out of what, into what?" It is the living stream of individual growth, whose flow is augmented and deepened by aesthetic experience.

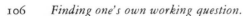

106   *Finding one's own working question.*

The purpose of art experience is not served by stirring up isolated little whirlpools of visual novelty, arrived at through prescribed manipulation of unusual media. Novel art materials and projects may help a teacher to capture children's attention and invite them to begin, but their crucial need is to go beyond beginning and to get into the work more deeply.

Creative working involvement requires a focusing which is given by the individual in positive response to his environment. Such aesthetic/creative responding means fusing one's own past seeing-and-feeling with one's present perception of environment through a process of stating choices; this experience will inevitably develop some basic individuality.

The whole lifelong process of responding consists of the increasingly probing questions which the individual asks of his environment and which his environment asks of him—back and forth, always more deeply. A teacher's job is to sense "out of what, into what" these questions flow and to help keep them workable in extent and in focus.

Work involvement can be helped by an understanding companion who says, in effect, "Listen," or "Look," or "Look again!"

A four-year-old child who had been impressed by an older brother's elaborate paper bag puppet picked up a paper bag and announced that she was going to make one like it. The teacher knew that the child was hardly ready to combine the operations of cutting, pasting, painting, and trimming, but did not interfere directly. Instead, when the child had turned to exploring cutting with scissors, the teacher said, "You cut very well with the scissors, Cathy." Cathy cut steadily across her crisp paper bag, and off came angular, floppy loops. She shook one out and thrust it over her arm. Another child said, "Hey, make me one," and soon children (and teacher) were prancing and parading with loops on heads, arms and legs.

4. Supporting

The teacher can *support* children's growth in aesthetic/creative experience by:

Giving them technical help when they ask or show a real need for it, and not before.

Helping children to face some degree of frustration if their work does not come "right" at once.

Helping children to study their own work, ask their own questions about it, see their own growth, and plan their next steps.

Children usually ask for technical help as part of working out a plan, rather than in planning itself. If much help of this kind is needed, the teacher will know that the activity is beyond the child's present ability. *If help is to support children's creative experiencing, it must not take that experiencing away from them.* Their requests for help can often be met best by asking questions which will clarify the problem they face. Sometimes suggesting a simplification of a plan or a detour of a problem will give the support needed. If direct intervention is necessary, as in fastening parts or thinning a paint, offering several solutions will help keep the work process open to the child's choosing. Referring him to impersonal aids, such as books or objects, may help to prevent a feeling of too great dependence on another individual.

The teacher's aim in giving help is to increase the child's confidence in his own perception of his materials, his own play with possibilities, his own planning, choosing, changing, and organizing. This confidence is built up gradually out of the child's independent seeing and saying, and the confidence he brings to any new venture represents his balancing of his successes against his failures.

What tests does the child apply in rating his aesthetic ventures as successful or unsuccessful? His first test is sensory pleasure in doing—a kind of "inner singing" concentration—and this pleasure ranges from the immediacy of sucking up the last strawful of creamy soda to response to tensions in relationships between visual events. Increased experience will enable the child to enjoy more subtle differences, but it is enjoyment which makes him seek the increased experience.

As a part or outgrowth of his doing, some kind of overt expression or product may emerge which he may then evaluate and to which others may respond. If based on clear observation and sympathetic understanding of the child's efforts, the teacher's recognition, encouragement, or praise can give strong support to a child's aesthetic/creative development. We know that certain kinds of praise or reward can also distort, subvert, or narrow creative efforts so that they will become calculated, competitive, or dependent. As with a medicine, the helpfulness of such comment depends on the need and condition of the organism. The test for the teacher is whether his praise or recognition will help the child to go ahead on his own, motivated by his pleasure in doing rather than by hunger for such praise. Since the teacher knows he is only one of many who may be affecting the child's aesthetic/creative development positively or negatively, he may see his role as that of a protagonist, who believes the child "has something" and wants very much to see him realize it. At the same time, the teacher knows that this realization depends on the child's increasing ability to evaluate his own actions and to plan his own next steps.

The child will need assurance of the right to fail occasionally as part of his creative venturing, and the teacher's long-term faith and realistic understanding can help him face these bad times, survive them, and go on to new efforts.

If a teacher himself has first-hand, continuous experience with creative working processes, he will sense when support means *not* to comment and not to comfort, for he will know that creative work demands a special kind of courage and stubborn honesty. And when he sees children come through with fresh, expressive surprises, he will celebrate not only the originality in their products but their growing trust in their own sensing and responding.

Questions

1. Since individual differences are basic to aesthetic experience and creative work, how can a teacher of a large class give effective help?
2. How does a teacher evaluate creative work of children on different developmental levels?

Appendix

Phases of Creative Process
and the Teacher's Supporting Role

1. *Preparation* or *Exploratory Play*. Experimenting with materials; active "questioning" without final commitment, predetermined goals, or "answers." An essential phase in all creative work and *the main activity of young children*.

   Teacher's Role. To help children "live with the question," make it their own; to support attentive play without distraction or pressure to avoid giving "answers"; to recognize imaginative quality in questioning; to focus on possibilities, keeping limits secondary.

2. *Incubation* or *Gestation*. From exploratory play a main question arises, becomes insistent. Failure to find a ready solution leads to a degree of frustration and to putting question aside, to be worked on by past experience and associations; this phase is noted by most great creators but is less clearly recognized in most children's work. Growing confidence in meeting some frustrations is needed in order to seek new solutions to harder questions. (Confidence is the product of generally successful ventures.)

   Teacher's Role. To be aware of this "child-at-work" phase; to avoid condemnation, impatience, over-comforting, or imposing ready-made answers; to help child to implant his own question, e.g., "Think it over and we'll come back to it later."

3. *Illumination* or *Insight*. Appearance of idea or plan. Creative workers report this usually as sudden, unexpected, and exciting relief (depending on the difficulty of the preceding search). Sometimes insight emerges completely formulated, sometimes only as a hunch. Children experience this, e.g., "I've got it!" "I have an idea!" or "Now I see!"

Teacher's Role. To recognize and value children's discoveries. In group projects, to help children respond to insights of all members rather than adopt the first idea or a plan of the more articulate; to try to include children's ideas in what is considered possible and relevant in the classroom.

4. *Working Out* or *Elaboration*. Stating or realizing new insights; giving it organized form within the requirements of medium and environment; making it communicable. This phase usually requires much conscious problem solving, some degree of technical mastery, and often adaptation to additional outside factors.

Teacher's Role. To give technical help when and as child needs it, without taking over his ideas and without making technique an end in itself. To help the child plan to carry out his ideas mostly within his present skills, mastering those techniques required by his inventive purposes.

How to Organize Found Materials
for Use in School Art Activities

Most of us who are teachers respond with interest to the words, *waste materials,* perhaps because of limited budgets, perhaps because our job is to see possibilities which others may have overlooked, in children, for example. The more positive term, *found materials,* suggests exploration, discovery, and perception. The materials may be found by a roadside or in a waste bin, or bought in dry goods and hardware stores. Finding them requires the ability to perceive, not merely to recognize and name.

How many materials should we provide for the child as he grows up? By the time he reaches kindergarten he is an experienced finder, and our job is more to go along with him in his explorations than merely to point out further possibilities. The teacher who is herself a finder will be able to offer such companionship.

Testing and Sharing New Materials

In many elementary schoolrooms, the discovery of materials is celebrated and shared in a *beauty corner,* where newly arrived leaves, ribbons, or other treasures can be honored with a favorable background and freed, from cluttered competition. A small collection of colored cloths, a few blocks or boxes, and a table screen, peg board or tack board to fasten things on, all set in adequate light, can facilitate the process and develop children's skills in exhibiting. They will learn to ask such questions as, "Does it look better on a dark background, hanging so the light shows through it, or . . . ?"

Usually, the finding of materials involves more than looking. Children need to play with the materials, giving them some degree of active try-out or test, for weight, texture, structure, silhouette, cross section, relation in repetition, and so on.

After the materials have been tested and shared, they may go into the classroom collection.

Sometimes children's search will be specially focused, as in finding things for printing or for making rubbings. If they find that their classroom found materials make their day-to-day work more interesting, they will be alert to new possibilities.

Collecting and Classifying

The experience of selecting, collecting, and using materials will be helped by classifying them according to their *design possibilities*. The number and names of classifications should be developed gradually with the children as they bring in their findings; these vary with age levels and interest. The following classification has been found useful in some classrooms:

1. *Spots and Dots*

    buttons, beads, tacks, bottle caps, flashbulbs, acorns, washers, marbles, pebbles, etc.

2. *Lines*

    a. *Stiff lines:* dowel sticks, bamboo, reeds, umbrella ribs, rods, applicator sticks, tooth picks, etc.

    b. *Controlled lines:* soft wires of annealed iron, copper, aluminum, solder, pipe cleaners, etc.

    c. *Free lines:* strings, yarns, ribbons, tapes, etc.

3. *Surfaces*

    a. *Stiff surfaces:* cardboard, coro-board, plywood, metal, etc.

    b. *Solid color surfaces:* papers (stored in portfolio, with separate folder for each family of colors); cloth (stored in box, cut pieces separate from longer ones).

    c. *Patterned surfaces:* wall paper sample books, gift wrappings, etc., in portfolio; patterned cloth in box.

    d. *Textured surfaces:* corrugated, waffle, metallic, sandpaper, roofing paper, shingles, etc., in portfolio; textured cloth in box.

    e. *See-through (translucent) surfaces:* screen, netting, cellophane, tissue, cheesecloth, plastic sheet, film, etc. ("light sifters").

4. *Textured stuffs*

steel wool, cotton, excelsior, shredded paper, raw fibers, flock, sawdust, shavings, etc. (in glass jars or plastic envelopes).

5. *Forms and Bases*

small cardboard boxes; wood cylinders, blocks, disks; yarn cones, spools, reels; styrofoam blocks and sheets, etc.

As the collection grows, sub-classifications may be added. For example, natural colored clays may start a row of Colors. The children will have many decisions to make as they sort and classify the materials they bring in. Is a paper doily a spot, a see-through surface, or a textured surface? Is old movie film a line or a see-through surface? Such deliberating is a useful step toward good design use of the materials.

Occasionally, collections need to be reduced and simplified, culling out materials which have proved to be too complex, too ready-made, or otherwise not useful.

Storage

Some reasonable, imaginative planning is necessary if a collection of materials is to be brought into the average classroom and kept available. Without carefully planned storage, complaints from building administrators can be expected; but more importantly, a careless jumbling can result in negative learnings by children—"This stuff doesn't matter." If the materials are worth collecting, they are worth careful sorting and storage. It is important that they be *"available"* (the children know them and know where they are) but that they also be *"once removed"* (meaning generally out of sight, put away, not distracting or demanding attention).

A practical way to solve these problems is to collect cartons, preferably of uniform size, and to paste wrapping paper over the printing on the outside. They should be labeled neatly and clearly (on both sides) with the agreed-upon classifications. Wooden apple boxes, painted and labeled, are portable and more durable than cartons. Since the boxes or cartons will be a part of the classroom's regular furnishings, it is wise to select and prepare them carefully. They can be lined up on a shelf, on tables, or on top of cupboards. In addition, consider what provision for collections of materials, such as fibreglass tote trays, or bins, and carts, should be provided in a new school building.

Within this orderly exterior, plan to isolate each material so that it can be located readily, with its special qualities visible. This calls for a collection of small cardboard boxes, covered plastic or glass jars, plastic bags, envelopes, paper bags, and rubberbands, as well as felt-brush markers and gummed tape for labeling. Some classrooms may have cupboard shelves for storage of jars and small boxes. Papers are best kept in cardboard portfolios or large envelopes, stored separately from cloth of the same classifications. Stiff lines may require a tall carton or can which stands in a corner. Coils of wire are more accessible if hung from peg-board hooks than if placed in a carton.

The children's committee which helps to manage the materials "library" may want to post on a bulletin board an index of samples or new additions.

Supplies and Tools

Working with a variety of materials requires supplies and tools for cutting, drilling, fastening, and other manipulation. These needs can be provided for simply or more completely, depending on the age of the children, the degree of interest, and the available resources; but a good range will facilitate work and reduce frustration and delay. In the following list, tools and supplies are named in approximate order of importance:

1. *Fastening*

   Adhesives: white glue; liquid paste; library paste; wallpaper paste flour; rubber cement in dispenser; airplane cement; masking tape, cellophane tape, and gummed kraft tapes.

   The children should learn how to use and care for adhesives. For example, all water-soluble pastes and glues (not rubber cement) cause shrinkage and warping. Paper which is pasted or painted with these will curl unless treated on both sides.

   Dry fastening: fine binding wire (30 to 36 gauge), straight pins, strings (carpet warp, etc.), thread (#60 and carpet thread, black and white), needles, paper clips, a combination stapler and tacker, rubber bands, a variety of small nails, light hammer, paper fasteners, spring clothes pins for clamping.

2. *Cutting*

   scissors, knives (pocket, Sloyd, stencil, mat knives), tin shears, wire cutting pliers, paper cutter, small model-maker's saw, jig saw, hack saw, single edge razor blades. Children should learn how to sharpen cutting edges.

   (Since scissors of young children are often inadequate for cutting cloth, precutting such materials in various small sizes may be necessary. The teacher should keep in her desk drawer better scissors and perhaps pinking shears and tin snips for hard-to-cut materials, such as carpet strips).

3. *Drilling*

   small hand drill with set of short twist drills; awl (nail in dowel-stick handle); paper or leather punches.

4. *Coloring and finishing*

water colors, dyes, stains, poster paints; brushes; shellac (and alcohol); clear plastic spray; enamels (and turpentine); lacquers (and lacquer thinner); liquid wax; linseed oil.

(When materials have been selected for their own qualities, it is usually a mistake to coat them with paint or shellac. Enamelling cork is like dressing an animal. Dyes, stains, or transparent water colors do less damage to texture but should be used with discrimination, usually for accent. The urge for shine and glitter is better satisfied with proper materials than with shellac, enamel, or gold paint. Sometimes oil or wax will help to restore or bring out the colors or grain of wood, stones, etc.)

5. *Materials for backgrounds and bases*

Collages: cardboards (laundry, carton materials, gift boxes), wall boards (insulation board, beaver board, masonite, plywood), waffle papers, corrugated paper, cloth, wall papers, colored papers, plastic sheet, etc.

Some wood strips may be needed for frames and supports—wood lath, lattice strips, garden stakes, etc. Small blocks of wood, cork, or styrofoam may help bring materials out from background.

Stabiles: some plastic materials which harden for bases and fastening, such as plaster (protect it from dampness in storage; in use, keep live plaster away from sink); clay mixed with yellow dextrine (1 tsp. per cup of clay), salt-paste, sawdust-paste mixtures. Wood blocks, disks, cardboard, styrofoam, small boxes, for bases.

6. *Lighting*

Providing an extension cord and perhaps a goose-neck desk lamp or reflector shade will make it possible for children to illuminate their work, dramatizing textures and form in collages, construction, space boxes, and dioramas.

Using a Materials Collection

In our present day economy, one can argue that it is more creative and productive to decide how far apart to space our mass-produced articles than it is to make things by hand. However, what is essential is that both craft products and space constructions become personal statements; this is achieved by the way one works with them.

A common approach to "waste materials" in the classroom is to turn them into ingenious representations of flowers, animals, dolls, or scenes. The value of these activities depends on the quality of individual discovery, perception, and imagination brought into play. In other words, the question is not so much *what* was made, but *who* planned and worked it out and *how* this work drew on the child's thinking/feeling experience.

The teacher's problem in managing *any* school materials is, of course, to help children focus on those working questions which will help them to learn. Their art work is directed toward enjoyment of visual relationships (seeing), and confidence in their own organizing and constructing (responding). Whether found materials will enhance such learning depends on the quality of children's participation in finding and trying out, and on the teacher's understanding and support of children's creative working processes.

Although working plans may develop directly out of experimenting with materials, usually they will grow out of some situational needs, such as a personal wish to "say" something, to change a particular setting, or to enhance some special occasion. Then, choosing materials may help one's expression of the fanciful, dramatic, delicate, grandiose, or austere quality which one has felt in the situation.

Children's work with found materials will develop into many kinds of projects, with media and processes elaborated, simplified, and combined to suit their own purposes. Included will be all kinds of collage, work with the discovered patterns of seeing through and imprinting, three-dimensional constructions which stand or hang, space constructions to be moved around and through; in fact, all of the *kinds* of work described in our adult Experiments and many others, but always adapted to the children's experience and interests.

What Kind of Help and Guidance?

In addition to sharing in the process of discovery, we can provide a free, relaxed, reasonable working climate. Since with children we know that exploring single materials or putting them together in simple associations may be more important than cutting and fashioning, we may provide paper and paste, or even a a range of clay, nails, or paper clips, but not a confusing array of materials at one time. At times the child will be engrossed in the mastery of such a skill as pasting or cutting. As he grows older, the child will achieve greater technical control. He will also be more subject to "good ideas," ready-made. Here we can help to nourish children's own resources by giving them access to rich, vivid experiences and by encouraging them to work in their own way. More by reference to their own life experiences than by design precepts or exercises, we can help them to see that it is usually better to avoid using many materials in one project; in such cases, the qualities would tend to blanket or drown each other out and result in confusion, rather than the intended meaning. With experience, children will learn to start with a main, theme material, bring in a supporting material if it is called for, and organize these on a background. A small shot of contrasting material may be effective. Each shift—up, down, forward, back—will offer a challenge for reconsideration, to which a child will respond according to his development and interest.

Setting forth such a process, step by step, with "rules" derived from adult analysis and intellectualization, can be a form of authoritarianism, applied to work process rather than to end product. It can also be guidance which will free creative powers if the teacher knows the children and is able to learn from them what questions they are ready to deal with. When teachers underrate the learnings of relationship offered by work with materials, they offer *no* guidance or companionship in selection or arrangement, and leave the child to such pressures as the products of older brothers, models in stores or on television, etc.

Adults who help children in their work with materials may find themselves re-examining their own values. An important part of the teacher's job will be to offer some consistent interpretation of children's efforts and learnings to parents and other out-of-the-classroom allies in the teaching process. In parents' meetings and in interpretive exhibits, the process can be emphasized and a preference for honest child expression can be built. For example, exhibiting some incomplete work of children may make clear their processes of choosing, planning, changing, and evaluating their work. This may be followed by enlisting parent help in finding useful materials for their children, and at the same time making clear why others are rejected as less useful, or harmful to children's learning. The pressure to seek "good public relations" by exhibiting or sending home dishonest art products can be countered only by developing increased respect and understanding for both children and parents. It is only on the strength of this mutual understanding that we can make the social aspects of classroom work with materials—as in "fixing the room," making gifts, preparing exhibits, making posters, or planning programs—positive contributions to the confidence which children may be building in more individual work. But materials can go into play whenever, in the individual or group life of the school, the appearance of things may be affected by the thought and feeling of children; they will be used well as children learn to make them a part of a well-understood visual vocabulary for saying "how it is."

COLLAPSIBLE PUPPET STAGE—For Hand Puppets

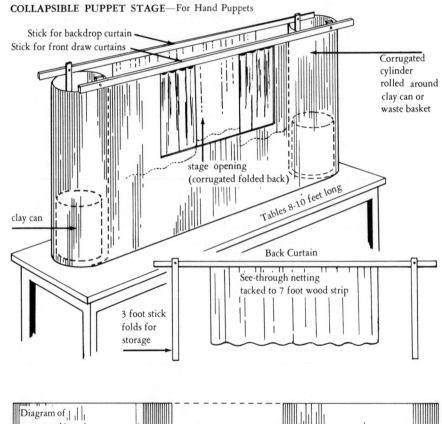

Stick for backdrop curtain

Stick for front draw curtains

Corrugated cylinder rolled around clay can or waste basket

stage opening (corrugated folded back)

clay can

Tables 8-10 feet long

Back Curtain

See-through netting tacked to 7 foot wood strip

3 foot stick folds for storage

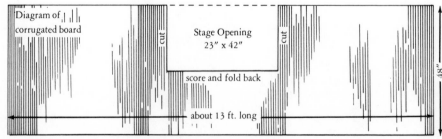

Diagram of corrugated board

cut

Stage Opening 23" x 42"

cut

score and fold back

48"

about 13 ft. long

Puppet Stages

A puppet stage aids the imagination by framing the puppet and hiding the operator. When operator and audience are combined in only one person, as in much of the child's playing, "staging" can be entirely imaginary. But the working together of two, three, five, or more participants, whether they be operators or audience, is usually facilitated by some kind of stage frame, however simple.

Collapsible Stage

A practical design for a collapsible puppet stage, suitable for classroom work with hand puppets, is shown on page 184. This stage, designed to stand on tables, can be assembled or taken down quickly, is easy to transport, and occupies little storage space. Besides the frame of the stage opening, it has a front draw curtain for beginning and ending an "act," and also a back curtain of netting to hide the operators' faces.

The stage is constructed of corrugated paper. This can be regular shipping grade, tan in color, which is obtainable from paper supply houses, or it can be window decorator's corrugated board, which comes in various colors but is somewhat less durable. The stage is held upright by rolling both ends of the corrugated board around empty clay cans or other cylindrical objects and fastening with paper clips. The front and back curtains are hung from long wooden strips set across the tops of the cylindrical ends of the stage and held in place by folding sticks hanging down inside the cylinders. The front draw curtain may be made of muslin, perhaps potato-printed by the children. Its curtain rings slide on the wire, which is tightly stretched over wood blocks and along the wooden strip (see below). The cords for opening and closing are run through screw eyes or pulleys and attached to the curtains as shown. Weights are sewn along the bottom hems.

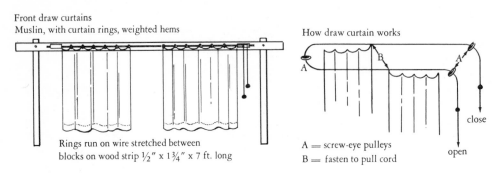

Front draw curtains
Muslin, with curtain rings, weighted hems

Rings run on wire stretched between
blocks on wood strip ½″ x 1¾″ x 7 ft. long

How draw curtain works

A = screw-eye pulleys
B = fasten to pull cord

close

open

The stage opening is provided by folding back the scored corrugated board as shown. Reinforcing all edges with gummed tape will make the stage more durable. The dimensions shown are suitable for taller children or adults. For smaller children, lower the stage opening, either by setting the stage on shorter-legged tables or by lowering the scored edge of the stage opening. This line should be about chest-high in relation to the operators.

Symbolic scenery, such as a tree, cloud, sign, or street light, can be cut out of paper or cardboard and pinned or hung on the net curtain backdrop, allowing operators to see through or around them to manage the puppets.

COMBINATION STAGE

For "Junk Puppetry"

(cross section)

**IMPROVISED
MARIONETTE STAGE**

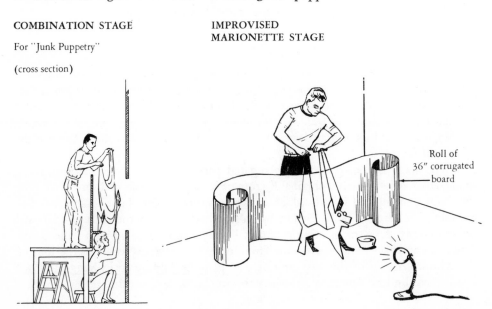

Roll of
36″ corrugated
board

Lighting can be provided most easily with a shaded lamp, held by a "light man" sitting out in front. Coat hangers covered with colored cellophane can add dramatic atmosphere to the lighting.

Dismantled and ready for storage, the stage consists of one package of curtains, rolled around their poles, and a second roll of the corrugated board.

Doorway Stage

A smaller stage can be set up easily in a doorway as shown here below. It consists of an opaque screen or curtain to cover the operators, either at head height or, if a net curtain backdrop is hung across the back of the door frame as shown, at chest height. Draw curtains would probably be omitted.

Such a doorway stage is easily adapted to shadow puppetry, with a strong light behind a flat translucent curtain, such as a bedsheet.

Marionette Stage

A simple marionette stage can be improvised out of a roll of 36″ corrugated cardboard. The operator stands behind this wall, and his marionette moves along the floor in front. A shaded lamp on the floor out in front will focus attention on the marionette.

Stage for "Junk Puppetry" Experiments

What is required for this kind of choreographed collage is a proscenium frame, the bottom edge of which is about 42″ above the floor. A masking screen or curtain surrounding the stage opening should be wide enough to hide the operators. The

DOORWAY STAGE—For Hand Puppets

For Shadow Puppets

(cross section)

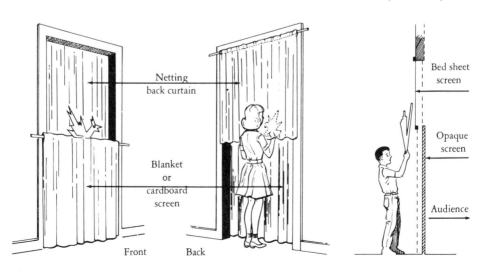

Netting back curtain

Blanket or cardboard screen

Front   Back

Bed sheet screen

Opaque screen

Audience

stage is equipped with a draw curtain like that on page 186. A stage backdrop should stand about 18″ behind the front screen and should be fastened to a stout table or workbench which serves as a platform for operators working from above the stage. Operators working from below may sit on a low bench or stools, and other operators may work from either end of the stage opening. The light source is above or at the ends of the stage. The stage itself will probably require either no floor at all or only a narrow, shelf-like board. The whole stage frame needs to be as adjustable as possible, with maximum freedom for collage movement and lighting behind the stage opening.

Making Photograms and Blueprints

The satisfaction in making photograms comes, of course, in finding your light-sifters and then in working out an arrangement of them which best uses their silhouette and translucent character and builds up to an exciting kind of composition.

You will need a dark-room equipped with the following:

A ruby light or safe light.

A desk lamp or other light source, 100 watts or less, for exposure of your photograms from about two feet away.

1 quart of Dektol developer (formerly called D-72). Use 1 part developer solution to 2 parts water.

1 gallon of hypo (solution from powder), enough to fill a tray.

A supply of single-weight, glossy, contact printing paper, kept protected from light. "Expired" paper will probably be satisfactory and is less expensive.

You can plan your photogram outside the darkroom, working with your light-sifter materials on a paper the size of your photo printing paper. The arrangement may be planned for a single light exposure or for several, with calculated time intervals for each part of the sequence. Those parts of your materials which press against the paper will be more sharply defined than those which are raised from the surface.

189

When your arrangement is worked out, carry it into the darkroom (perhaps on cardboard or a pane of glass), transfer it to printing paper, expose, develop, and wash it. Exposure should be from three to four seconds. Make test strips. Bathe the print in the developer and follow with a ten minute bath in a tray of hypo and one-half hour of washing in running water.

Blueprints are less sensitive and require less careful handling than photograms. The objects to be printed should be held close to the paper under glass during exposure to the light. This is best done in a printing frame with glass front and removable back.

Different kinds of blueprint paper are available and call for different treatment, but the usual practice is to expose the blueprint to strong sunlight for one and one-half to two minutes, then wash in clear water, moving occasionally, until the paper turns blue, and white lines or patterns appear. If white design does not show, try a different amount of exposure.

A clearer, sharper blueprint will result if the exposed print is first dipped into a solution of potassium dichromate and water (one ounce to two gallons of water) and then washed thoroughly in clear water. In working with children, omit this dipping process.

Children's Clay Work

For children of all ages, clay offers unique expressive advantages. Its responsiveness to the touch and pressure of hands and fingers provides a tactile pleasure and directness of three-dimensional statement which is quite different from working on a flat surface with crayons or paints. Children learn that clay must be used honestly and sympathetically, with patient, attentive handling.

The following notes are offered to teachers as a supplement to their first-hand experience with clay. Through the understanding gained from such personal experience, we can move from "administering" clay work to helping children. We will know that the first requirement for clay work is that it be one's own, that step-by-step following of directions is out of place here, and that working with clay is a two-way process—"We tell the clay, and the clay tells us."

But how can we make clay work possible in our classrooms?

Clay

Because of its tactile qualities, the best clay to use is moist modeling clay, called ball clay, buff-firing clay, or Jordan clay. It can be bought in 50-pound metal cans or in fiber containers lined with pliofilm. In either form it will stay in good condition as long as it is protected from air. Dry clay flour is more economical, but preparing it by hand is time consuming.

Children should be taught how to remove the lid of a clay can, with hammer and woodblock, without bending it out of shape. Individual portions are most easily prepared by cutting the clay with a fine wire.

Clay Storage

For classroom storage of clay, a covered garbage can or a large covered pickle jar is good. When a child returns a ball of clay to the can, he can poke a hole in the top of the ball and put a little water in it to restore it to good working consistency. This consistency must be kept just right if children are to have the best experience from clay work. Test clay by wrapping a coil around your finger to see that it neither sticks to your fingers nor cracks. If clay gets too wet, it should be spread out or worked on an absorbent surface. The best is a dry slab of plaster; dry potato sacks or other heavy cloth or unfinished wood are also adequate. If the clay is too dry, work it on these same surfaces after soaking them with water, or spread out the clay, wet the surface, roll it up, and knead in the water.

Restoring Dried Clay

Dried clay can be restored to good working condition. Pieces containing paint, grease, wire, or wood should be discarded. In a stout wooden box the dried clay is pounded and churned, a little at a time, with a ball bat, pole, or mallet until the clay is reduced to a powder. In a pail or can this powder is covered with water and allowed to stand for several days. Then the water is poured off and the thick, wet clay poured out on an absorbent surface. It will soon be ready to roll up and use. A school which uses much clay will find that a plaster-topped table surrounded by a low wooden wall will make this drying out easy. A committee of upper grade children can carry out this whole process.

In summer camps the discovery and preparation of local "ditch" clay is an interesting activity. This is done by soaking the clay in a large barrel or tank, stirring and straining the watery mixture and allowing it to settle. Then pouring off the water reveals a layer of good clay, separated from sand and other impurities. Because its contents and plasticity will vary greatly, such natural clay is not recommended for school use.

Storing Unfinished Work

After the primary years, children may wish to work on clay projects for more than one period. The best solution for storing damp work is an old ice box. If its shelves are equipped with thick plaster slabs (cast in a greased baking pan), they will hold enough moisture to keep clay work damp without being covered. Keep paper and wood out of this "damp box." If there is no space for an ice box in or near the classroom, store unfinished work in wide-mouthed cans with tight covers or in plastic bags.

Working Surfaces

Floor tiles of asphalt, rubber, or linoleum are good to work on, as are plaster bats (cast in pie tins). Hardware stores sell galvanized iron in pieces about 5″ x 7″ for roofing repairs. Enameled boards 8″ or 10″ square work well. Some kind of non-absorbent board is essential so that the clay work can be turned. The child's work may also be helped by raising it to his eye level occasionally on a turntable, can, or box, so that he can get a new view of his work.

Tools

The best tools for clay work are our hands. Tongue depressors may be useful in more advanced work, but not at the start. From ⅜″ or ½″ birch dowel sticks, older children can file and sandpaper other modeling tools for detailed work. Wire loop tools are useful for hollowing out thick pieces for firing, but a strip of bent metal or a loop of stiff wire will suffice. With a rolling pin, ½″ thick strips of wood, and a piece of dampened muslin, slabs for tiles, "fossils," or space constructions can be rolled out.

Clean-up

The other requirements for clay work are water, whether in a sink or pail, and sponges or rags for cleaning up. (It is better not to make water available during clay modeling, since this encourages slick surfaces and tactile experience rather than shaping.) Giving children a few practical instructions about cleanup will help to avoid strained relations with custodians: (1) Keep clay in two pieces—the work and the extra clay supply. (2) Use a piece of clay to collect crumbs lest they fall to the floor and get on the soles of shoes, to be printed far and wide. (3) Examine your shoe soles before leaving the room. (4) In cleaning up, sweep before you scrub. Scrape or brush crumbs toward the middle of the table to be picked up in a dust pan. A surface scrubbed over with water *and* clay will dry with a gray film. It should be dried with a wrung-out sponge or a squeegee. (5) A final guarantee of institutional spotlessness can be provided quickly by a cloth treated with paraffin oil.

Not Only Clean

These instructions for clean-up may sound forbidding, and indeed they might be if used in introducing clay work. However, after the satisfaction of a good work experience with clay, this procedure will seem reasonable and simple enough to most children.

Our evaluation of children's clay work will be in the doing, in whether they have made *their own* products, whether these are "happy," clay-like pieces of work, and whether they show growing self-confidence in three-dimensional expression—how the shape stands up, to be seen all around, and how it holds together visually.

Firing Clay

Firing in a kiln converts fragile clay pieces into permanent, waterproof pottery. The work of young children is seldom fired for the children's sake. Firing it for their adult friends is likely to be accompanied by other production pressures which may detract from the value of the experience. A kindergarten teacher firing rows of hand-prints is probably a martyr to mistaken public relations.

As children achieve greater mastery in their clay modeling, the possibility of firing their products can enrich and fulfill the experience of clay work. This stage is probably reached when children can really understand and to some extent share in the firing process.

For most schools, electric kilns with automatic temperature controls and shutoff are usually most practical. Their cost and small capacity limit the size and number of pieces which can be fired.

If it is to be fired, clay work must be made with care. It must contain no air pockets and should have thick parts hollowed out while still moist, either from below or by cutting work in half with a thin wire, hollowing the halves, and fastening them together with clay slip (a creamy mixture of clay and water).

The first firing (to about 1900°) produces a "biscuit ware" which, while some-what absorbent, is washable and strong. Its color, from buff to pink or red, depends on the amount of iron in the clay. Decoration can be applied with colored clay slips or with underglaze colors (not paints) before refiring.

Glazing requires a second firing to melt and fuse a coat of colored glass over the surface of the piece. Instructions for this and for other ceramic processes are available in potters' handbooks. For a bowl, vase, or ash tray to have utilitarian value, it must be fired and glazed in order to hold water and be cleaned easily.

Painting Clay

Painting, enamelling, or shellacking clay makes a potter shudder. Like enamel-ing pine cones, it adds a skin or scum which hides the quality of the material. How-ever, at times, adding poster paint, a stain of water color, or a coat of liquid wax to clay figures or models is justifiable; and young children, not ready for ceramic pro-cesses, may even add sticks, wire, beads, and all manner of things to their clay work.

Shrinkage

The teacher needs to remember that clay shrinks on drying. Clay covering a board to make a model or map will probably crack as it shrinks, as will clay wrapped around wires, sticks, or tin cans. If a dried clay animal loses a tail, it cannot be re-placed with wet clay as it will shrink off in drying. The whole piece must be softened so that the addition will be of the same consistency.

Helping Children in Clay Work

With children there should be no step-by-step instructions, no models or demonstrations of production; the experienced teacher can share with children her enjoyment of clay's qualities without imposing her ideas, and she can recognize the expressiveness of what the children are making and how they make it. She will also sense when work should continue uninterrupted and when it is time to stop work.

Usually the clay will go back into the clay can, but sometimes all of the products may march along on a high shelf, safe from accidents, to celebrate the wealth of the class's variety.

As children seek greater mastery of the medium, the teacher can show them how to join pieces securely by the use of slip. She can help children to honor the material by using its special qualities and not forcing it into hard, thin, picky forms unsuited to it. She can help older children to share their discoveries of contrasting textures, round, full forms against flat or hollow forms, and what makes pieces "hang together" or interesting from all views. But this will be done when needed, without preaching rules or assigning exercises. Fresh beginnings will come from children's observations and experiences, as in feeling the curve of their own bending backs or the snug curling-up for sleep. Along with recognition of their own progress, children will learn from seeing the quality possible in the work of the master, through watching him at work in his own studio or through seeing his products in galleries or museums.

Other Modeling Media

Plasticene contains oil instead of water, so it never hardens and can be used repeatedly. It is made in colors, with gray or green usually preferred. It offers fewer cleanup problems but less tactile satisfaction and, more importantly, less responsiveness in shaping than clay. Since it does not shrink, it is good for relief maps and models or for figures built around wire or sticks for dioramas, models, etc. Before being painted with poster paints, plasticene should be dipped in shellac. Although it softens with handling, old, used plasticene may need to have paraffin or castor oil added and be run through a food chopper.

Clay with Dextrine. Adding one part of yellow dextrine (from druggist) to about twenty parts of clay and kneading it thoroughly will produce a material almost as strong as fired clay although it will not be waterproof. Mix only enough for immediate use. It dries better in fairly thin pieces.

Sawdust and Paste and *Salt and Paste.* Use one part of wallpaper flour paste to five or six of sawdust or salt. A little alum will prevent mold. These mixtures may be used for puppet heads, small models, or relief maps. They shrink, but crack less than clay.

A *Dough* of flour and salt, using much less salt than in the above mixture, is more pleasant to the touch but not suited for permanent products. It is used in pre-school housekeeping centers, with measuring cups, cookie cutters, etc. Do not confuse it with clay. Wallpaper cleaner and ready-made play doughs are pleasant materials for young fingers.

Papier Mâché is made by soaking torn-up bits of newsprint or other soft, absrob-ent paper and adding paste. It is useful for maps, models, puppet heads, etc. If too thick, it may mold in drying, so it is better applied a layer at a time or built over a core of cardboard or wood. Larger constructions are better made by pasting sheets of newspaper covered with wallpaper paste over some kind of built-up base.

Various *Self-hardening Clays,* or clays which can be baked in a kitchen oven, are offered by art stores. These are expensive for regular class use, but suitable for small scale work such as costume jewelry.

All the above modeling materials have their uses and advantages and are worth experimenting with. None is a really good substitute for clay.

Criteria for Planning Children's Creative Art Projects Which Are Related to Other Curriculum Areas

It is assumed that most of the children's art experiences will be planned primarily for creative expression, with other learnings valued as secondary. The following questions are among those which a teacher might ask herself in planning art work with subject material based in science, social studies, literature, etc.

How direct, vivid, and personal is the child's experience with the subject, topic, or content? Are his seeing and questioning likely to be first-hand, or must he depend on others' seeing and questioning?

Is there evidence that the children are ready and able, intellectually and emotionally, to work with this subject material? Is it reasonable to expect some basic, conceptual understanding of it at this stage?

Is the child able to identify himself with the central subject area or content? Does he respond to it with feeling, or does he respond primarily to the adult's feeling about it?

Is the child's work on the project likely to arouse some feeling of personal wonder, of the extraordinary or special, or will its primary result be acceptance of prescribed information or increase in manipulative skills?

Does the plan for work emphasize, "This is how *it* is," or "This is how it is *to me*"? Will children's work tend to look alike, conforming to some objective model, or can it reflect the unique experience and interests of individual children?

Does aesthetic response to the subject area suggest the use of only one medium? Might a variety be drawn upon naturally?

Does the plan depend on children's interest in the *experience* (to be expressed) or in the *medium* (of expression)?

Will the project invite *each* child to raise his own questions?

What can the child do to find answers to his questions? Are suitable resources accessible for his investigations?

Do plans call for the use of unfamiliar media, tools, materials, processes? Are these suited to the use of these children? Will some (too much?) guided introductory experience be necessary before they can be used independently?

Do plans have sufficient range to provide possibilities of good creative experiences for each child, or will some be only helpers or busy-workers?

Is the main, creative part of the plan the teacher's "framework" (to be carried out or filled in by the children), or will the main, creative part be the children's work (supported by the teacher's framework)?

Is the plan worked out in advance, to be executed by the children according to step-by-step instructions, or is much of the plan worked out together, with the children really exploring, questioning, thinking over possibilities, with the teacher guiding them toward practical realization of their ideas?

What are the main measures of "success" which are implied by the plan?

On Experimenting with Mobiles

Clear examples of expressive statement through related movement are found in the mobiles of Alexander Calder. What a mobile has to say, what it is all about, is usually ignored in commercial adaptations for decoration or for children's construction. Just as in puppetry "it's not the thing, it's the wiggle," so in mobiles the individuality of the "things" is unimportant compared to the variability of their relationship in movement.

A mobile should be studied as a system of *infinitely variable positional relationships in space*. This suggests why the hanging of cut-out shapes from opposite ends of a suspended coat hanger produces a lifeless mobile. It also suggests directions for possible development in adult study:

Differentiating air-catching *sails* (planes of cardboard, etc.) from heavier, more compact, *counterweights* (as in a weathervane), and reducing the fancy solo quality of both.

Varying the sweep of orbits by adjusting the length of *horizontal arms* (wire, sticks, or reed).

Using cantilever of off-center hanging and balancing sails with weights.

Seeking a maximum variety of *vertical axes* (threads or strings) and avoiding the monotony of lining up one axis above another; balancing one axis with a set of sub-axes; varying levels of movement through lengths of axis threads.

Planning for narrow escapes and near misses, as well as distant responses of almost unrelated movement.

199

To begin construction, arrange on a table your chosen elements (sails, arms, weights and axes) and assemble by tying threads (axes) to your extending sticks or wires (arms) with temporary knots, to allow for later adjustment. Tie a paper clip hook to the top thread, for easy hanging, trying out, and taking down of your mobile.

Mobiles are usually thought of in terms of their side view, but the true test of a mobile is in its top or bottom view, revealing all the variations of swinging, approaching, or departing orbits or sub-orbits which are possible for that mobile. Therefore, most of the work must be done when the mobile is hanging. Most of the adjustment of balances and counterbalances must begin at the bottom of the mobile. When the desired movement has been worked out, fasten each knot on the thread axes with a drop of glue.

These suggestions are for experimentation with free swinging mobiles, whose parts may turn 360 degrees on their axes. Another kind allows only limited movement of its parts. Instead of thread axes, two wire loops are linked together, permitting restricted movement as in vertebrae or in leaves. The free swinging type with thread axes is usually preferable for beginning experimentation.

Study of a mobile should lead to looking for and responding to mobile-like, related movements in the environment. Examples of "infinitely variable positional relationships in space" can be found on a playground observed from above, in a basketball game, in an aquarium or fish pond, or in interstellar space. Others can be seen in the imagination, as in the varied moving overhead within an apartment building, or, in a more personal sense, in those moments during a working day when we correlate our own present actions with the imagined moving of absent loved ones. Indeed, it is in the context of our "moving" along paths which converge and separate that we experience some of our deepest feelings.

The best way to develop understanding of the related movements of a mobile is to join with a group to work out a dance movement in varying relationship to each other. Although ropes or poles can be used to maintain distance from moving centers, the connection of subordinate moving relationships can also be imagined and felt.

Supplementary Reading

Chapter 2

Fleming, Robert S., ed. *Curriculum for Today's Boys and Girls.* Columbus: Charles E. Merrill Publishing Company, 1963. Chapter 13 and 6-page bibliography on Creativity, by Gladys Andrews.

Ghiselin, Brewster, ed. *The Creative Process.* New York: Mentor Books, 1958.

Kaufman, Irving. *Art and Education in Contemporary Culture.* New York: The Macmillan Company, 1966. Chapter 15, "Redirection in Art Education."

MacKinnon, Donald W. "What Makes a Person Creative," *Saturday Review* (Feb. 10, 1962).

Rugg, Harold. *Imagination.* New York: Harper & Row, 1963.

Chapter 3

Arnheim, Rudolf. *Art and Visual Perception.* Berkeley: University of California Press, 1954.

Fleming, Robert S., ed. *Curriculum for Today's Boys and Girls.* Columbus: Charles E. Merrill Publishing Company, 1963. Chapter 5, "Exploring the World, Discovering Self," by Frances Minor.

Chapter 4

Dienes, Sari. "Unconventional Use of Print Techniques," *Craft Horizons,* March-April, 1956.

Dillon, E. V. *Early New England Gravestone Rubbings.* New York: Dover Publications, Inc., 1966

Chapter 5

Baranski, Matthew. *Graphic Design: a Creative Approach.* Scranton: International Textbook Co., 1960.

Heller, John. *Print Making Today.* New York: Holt, Rinehart & Winston, Inc., 1958.

Mattil, Edward L. *Meaning in Crafts.* Englewood Cliffs: Prentice-Hall Inc., 1959. pp. 36-40.

Myers, Hans. *One Hundred Fifty Techniques in Art.* New York: Reinhold Publishing Corp., pp. 36-40.

Ota, Koshi, et al., *Printing for Fun.* New York: McDowell, Ivan Obolensky, Inc., 1960.

Voss, Gunther. *Craft and Hobby Book.* New York: Reinhold Publishing Corp., pp. 148-150.

Chapter 6

Ball, Carlton and Janice Lovoos. *Making Pottery without a Wheel: Texture and Form in Clay.* New York: Reinhold Publishing Corp., 1965.

The Museum of Modern Art. *Texture and Pattern: Portfolio No. 2* E. C. Osborn, ed. New York: The Museum of Modern Art, 1949.

Chapter 7

Feininger, Andreas. *The Anatomy of Nature.* New York: Crown Publishers, Inc., 1956.

Kepes, Gyorgy. *The Language of Vision.* Chicago: Paul Theobald, 1944.

Chapter 8

Janis, Harriet and Rudi Blesh. *Collage:Personalities, Concepts. Techniques.* Philadelphia: Chilton Book Company, 1962.

Lord, Lois. *Collage and Construction in Elementary and Junior High Schools.* Worcester, Mass.: Davis Publications, Inc., 1958.

Seitz, William. *Art of Assemblage.* New York: Museum of Modern Art, 1962.

Chapter 9

Copland, Aaron. *What to Listen for in Music.* New York: Mentor Books, 1953.

Sessions, Roger. *The Musical Experience of Composer, Performer, Listener.* Princeton: Princeton University Press, 1958.

Sheehy, Emma D. *Children Discover Music and Dance.* New York: Holt, Rinehart & Winston, Inc., 1959.

Chapter 10

Baird, Bil. *The Art of the Puppet.* New York: The Macmillan Company, 1966.

Board of Education, New York City. *Puppetry in the Curriculum.* Curriculum Bulletin No. 1, 1948.

Pratt, Lois H. *The Puppet Do-It-Yourself Book.* New York: Exposition Press, 1957.

Chapter 12

Duncan, Julia H. and Victor D'Amico. *How to Make Pottery and Ceramic Sculpture.* New York: Museum of Modern Art, 1947.

Read, Herbert. *The Art of Sculpture.* New York: Pantheon Books, Inc., 1965.

Robertson, Seonaid. *Rosegarden and Labyrinth: a Study in Art Education.* New York: Barnes & Noble, Inc., 1963.

Röttger, Ernst. *Creative Clay Design.* New York: Reinhold Publishing Corp., 1965.

Museum of Modern Art. *Modern Art Old and New: Teaching Portfolio No. 3.* René d'Harnoncourt, ed., New York: Museum of Modern Art, 1950.

_____. *Modern Sculpture: Teaching Portfolio No. 1.* E. C. Osborn, ed., New York: Museum of Modern Art, 1947.

Chapter 13

Klee, Paul. *Pedagogical Sketchbook.* New York: Frederick A. Praeger, Inc. 1953.

Lord, Lois. *Collage and Construction.* Worcester, Mass.: Davis Publications, Inc., 1958.

Nicolaides, Kimon. *The Natural Way to Draw.* Boston: Houghton Mifflin Company, 1941.

Chapter 14

Andrews, Gladys. *Creative Rhythmic Movement for Children.* Englewood Cliffs: Prentice-Hall Inc., 1954.

Drew, Elizabeth. *Poetry: a Modern Guide to Its Understanding and Enjoyment.* New York: Dell Publishing Co., Inc., 1959.

Greenberg, Pearl. *Children's Experiences in Art: Drawing and Painting.* New York: Reinhold Publishing Corp., 1966.

Kaupelis, Robert. *Learning to Draw.* New York: Watson-Guptill Publications, 1966.

Nicolaides, Kimon, *The Natural Way to Draw.* Boston: Houghton Mifflin Co., 1941.

Robertson, Seonaid. *Rosegarden and Labyrinth: a Study in Art Education.* New York: Barnes & Noble, Inc., 1963.

Roth, Henry. *Call It Sleep.* New York: Avon Books, 1964.

Chapter 15

Itten, Johannes. *The Art of Color.* New York: Reinhold Publishing Corp., 1961.

Petterson, Henri, and Ray Gerring. *Exploring Painting.* New York: Reinhold Publishing Corp.

Janson, H. W., and D. J. Janson. *The Picture History of Painting.* New York: Harry N. Abrams, Inc., 1957.

Chapter 16

Healy, Frederick. *Light and Color.* New York: The John Day Company, Inc., 1962.

Chapter 17

Bachelard, Gaston. *The Poetics of Space.* New York: Orion Press, 1964.

Feininger, Lyonel. *City at the Edge of the World.* New York: Frederick A. Praeger, Inc., 1965.

Kephart, Newell C. *The Slow Learner in the Classroom.* Columbus: Charles E. Merrill Publishing Company, 1960.

Lynch, Kevin. *The Image of the City.* Cambridge: Harvard University Press, 1960.

Chapter 18

Johnson, Pauline. *Creating with Paper.* Seattle: University of Washington Press, 1958.

Kiesler, Frederick. *Inside the Endless House.* New York: Simon and Schuster, Inc., 1966.

Mumford, Lewis, ed. *Roots of Contemporary Architecture.* New York: Reinhold Publishing Corp., 1952.

Röttger, Ernst. *Creative Wood Design.* New York: Reinhold Publishing Corp., 1961.

Chapter 19

Miel, Alice, ed., *Creativity in Teaching: Invitations and Instances.* San Francisco: Wadsworth Publishing Co., 1961.

Strom, Robert D., ed., *The Inner-City Classroom: Teacher Behaviors.* Columbus: Charles E. Merrill Publishing Company, 1966. "Fostering Creative Behavior," by E. Paul Torrance. pp. 57-75.

On teaching art in elementary schools:

Barkan, Manuel. *Through art to Creativity: Art in the Elementary School Program.* Boston: Allyn & Bacon, Inc., 1961.

Bland, Jane Cooper. *Art of the Young Child, from Three to Five Years.* New York: Museum of Modern Art, 1957.

Conant, Howard and Arne Randall. *Art in Education.* Peoria, Ill.: Chas. A. Bennett Co., Inc., 1959.

D'Amico, Victor. *Creative Teaching in Art.* Scranton: International Textbook Co., 1954.

Erdt, Margaret H. *Teaching Art in the Elementary School.* New York: Holt, Rinehart, & Winston, Inc., 1954.

Gaitskell, C. D. *Children and Their Art: Methods for the Elementary School.* New York: Harcourt, Brace & World, Inc., 1958.

Jefferson, Blanche. *Teaching Art to Children.* Boston: Allyn & Bacon, Inc., 1959.

Lark-Horovitz, B., Hilda Lewis, Marc Luca. *Understanding Children's Art for Better Teaching.* Columbus: Charles E. Merrill Publishing Company, 1967.

Lindstrom, Miriam. *Children's Art.* Berkeley: University of California Press, 1957.

Lowenfeld, Viktor. *Your Child and His Art.* New York: Macmillan Co., 1956.

———— and W. L. Brittain. *Creative and Mental Growth.* New York: The Macmillan Co., 1964.

Mattil, Edward L. *Meaning in Crafts.* Englewood Cliffs: Prentice-Hall, Inc., 1959.

McFee, June King. *Preparation for Art.* San Francisco: Wadsworth Publishing Co., 1961.

McIlvaine, Dorothy. *Art for the Primary Grades.* New York: G. P. Putnam's Sons, 1961.

Mendelowitz, Daniel. *Children Are Artists.* Stanford: Stanford University Press, 1953.

Index